Portuguese Country Inns & Pousadas

BOOKS IN KAREN BROWN'S COUNTRY INN SERIES

AUSTRIAN COUNTRY INNS & CASTLES

ENGLISH, WELSH & SCOTTISH COUNTRY INNS

EUROPEAN COUNTRY CUISINE - ROMANTIC INNS & RECIPES

FRENCH COUNTRY INNS & CHATEAUX

GERMAN COUNTRY INNS & CASTLES

ITALIAN COUNTRY INNS & VILLAS

PORTUGUESE COUNTRY INNS & POUSADAS

SPANISH COUNTRY INNS & PARADORS

SWISS COUNTRY INNS & CHALETS

Scheduled for 1987

IRISH COUNTRY INNS & COTTAGES

SCANDINAVIAN COUNTRY INNS & MANORS

Portuguese Country Inns & Pousadas

CYNTHIA & RALPH KITE

Illustrated by

BARBARA TAPP

TRAVEL PRESS   San Mateo, California

Illustrations, Cover Design & Painting: Barbara Tapp
Maps: Keith Cassell

TRAVEL PRESS editors: Karen Brown, Clare Brown, CTC, June Brown, CTC, Cynthia Kite, Ralph Kite, Iris Sandilands; distribution: Kimberly Brown

This book is written as a publication for:

Town and Country Travel Service
16 East Third Avenue, San Mateo, California 94401

International Standard Book Number: 0-930328-19-1
Library of Congress Catalog Card Number: 86-050177
Printed in the United States of America

Travel Press   San Mateo, California

Distributed in the United States by:
MACMILLAN PUBLISHING COMPANY

Distributed in Canada by:
COLLIER MACMILLAN CANADA, INC

For Pete and Viddie

Companions in More Than Travel

Contents

HOTEL SECTION

INDEXES

Introduction

A favorite concept of the Portuguese is the sentiment they call SAUDADE. No precise translation exists, though Portuguese poets have tried to portray it in many ways over the centuries with varying degrees of success. In the simplest terms, "to have saudade" means to miss someplace, something or someone you love - but it's a bittersweet longing because, somehow, the lack of what you love becomes closely linked with the loving, and the memory is the point. Anyway, it's what you'll feel after you have visited Portugal, just as it's what all Portuguese feel when they are somewhere else. It's thought to be a uniquely Portuguese sentiment because so many of them have spent so much of their lives somewhere else.

Portugal's history is irrevocably tied to the sea. Its most glorious period was the 15th century, when the Portuguese discovered and developed the coveted sea route to the Orient and monopolized the spice trade. At the same time Columbus was discovering a New World, Bartolomeu Dias and Vasco da Gama were testing the frontiers in the opposite direction - Africa, India and the East Indies. Brazil, now one of the largest countries in the world, was incidental at the time. So a lot of Portuguese have spent a lot of time with saudade for their homeland, a tiny, southwestern corner of the European continent, and you'll understand why when you've seen it.

ABOUT THIS GUIDE

Our goal has been to discover and describe the most charming and historic hotels in Portugal and to detail itineraries which will lead you to them by the most scenic and interesting routes. This book may not appeal to everyone. It is designed for the traveller looking for a guide to more than the capital city and a handful of highlights - for the visitor who wants to add a little out of the ordinary to his agenda. We do not claim to be objective reporters - that sort of treatment is available anywhere - but rather subjective, on-site raconteurs. We have definite biases toward hotels we have visited and enjoyed - from tiny hotels in ancient castles to lavish and lovely hotels overlooking the Atlantic. We believe that your choice of accommodations may weave the tapestry of your trip. They can make or break a visit to any country, and can add immeasurably to your memories. And prices in Portugal are still reasonable enough to allow you the pleasure of indulging yourself. If you follow our itineraries (every one of which we have personally travelled) and trust in our hotel recommendations, you will be assured of staying in the most interesting lodging Portugal has to offer while visiting the country's most intriguing destinations.

BANKS

The unit of currency in Portugal is the "escudo" and, in mid-1986, the exchange rate was about 147 to the U.S. dollar. Large newspapers carry current exchange rates, should you want to check it near the time of your departure. Banks in Portugal are open from 9:00 a.m. to 1:00 p.m., then again from 2:30 to 3:30 p.m., Monday through Friday. Some, usually in larger towns, maintain morning business hours on Saturday. Many, but not all, exchange foreign currency; look for a CAMBIO (exchange) sign outside the bank. Often, your hotel will exchange your dollars, though usually at a slightly less-favorable rate.

CAR RENTAL

This guide is the perfect companion for the traveller who wants to experience Portugal by car. We can suggest one international car-rental agency which we have found to be especially reasonable and dependable, the Kemwell Group, though you may have your particular favorite. Their phone number is: 800 468-0468. If you are planning a lengthy trip, you might want to consider buying a car in Europe and shipping it home; it's surprisingly uncomplicated if you arrange the purchase in the United States (check with your local foreign car dealer for details).

CLIMATE

Portugal enjoys Europe's best climate since the moderating influence of the Atlantic keeps all seasons relatively mild in most parts of the country. There is a natural progression of temperature variation from the north to the south. It is seldom hot in the north and almost never cold in the Algarve. The highest and lowest temperatures show greater divergence as you move away from the coast and, in the higher mountain ranges such as the SERRA DA ESTRELA, there is enough snow for skiing in winter. In most of the country winter most often means simply an increase in rainfall.

CLOTHING

As holds true throughout Europe, standard attire is generally less casual than in the United States. Although women wear slacks just about anywhere they would at home, dresses are most often seen in the evening, and short shorts are rarely seen outside the tourist-intensive coastal resorts. Men in Portugal dress noticeably more formally than men elsewhere. While ties and jackets are actually required in only the most elegant establishments, you will find that they are worn regularly.

CREDIT CARDS

Many hotels in Portugal accept plastic payment. All pousadas accept all major cards. A few very small places accept none at all. In the hotel descriptions we indicate which hotels accept which cards with the following abbreviations: AX = American Express, VS = Visa, MC = Master Card (called Eurocard in Europe), DC = Diner's Club or, simply, "all major".

CURRENT

You will need a transformer plus an adapter if you plan to take an American-made electrical appliance. Even if the appliance is dual-voltage, as many of them are these days, you'll still need an adapter plug. The voltage is usually 220, but occasionally a 110 outlet is provided in the hotel bathroom. These outlets are meant for electric razors only and they usually can't handle the demand of a hair dryer, for example. These outlets usually also require an adapter plug. Be sure to check with the manager if the outlet is not clearly marked.

DRIVING

DRIVER'S LICENSE: Portugal requires only that you have a valid driver's license from your home country.

GASOLINE: Gasoline is quite expensive (more than double the U.S. price) and should be considered in your budget if you plan to drive extensively. It is a price-regulated item, so it will cost the same everywhere. Gasoline is available in almost any town, and service stations are open from around 7:00 a.m. to at least 10:00 p.m. A few are open 24 hours a day. Using a little common sense, you should have no trouble finding gasoline.

ROADS: Roads in Portugal run the gamut from good national highways to barely two-lane country roads (and, as you might expect, our countryside itineraries find you more often on the latter). There are, at present, only a few short stretches of freeway around the major cities. We figured that, on all but a few national highways, we averaged under 50 kilometers per hour during our travels. Passing through small towns and sharing the road with trucks, horse or ox carts, mopeds and pedestrians make it difficult to beat that average, but the leisurely pace allows you time to enjoy the surroundings as you drive. The country's character doesn't lend itself to your being in a hurry, and neither do the itineraries, because we have taken that into account. If you foresee a long-day's drive and haven't hotel reservations already, simply call in the morning to the hotel you plan to visit that evening, make a reservation, stating you'll be arriving late (reservations are routinely held until 6:00 or 7:00 p.m. unless otherwise arranged), then relax and enjoy your day.

Road numbers in Portugal are not always reliable indications of their quality. Generally, the lower the number preceded by N, the better the road (e.g., N1 is the main route from Lisbon to Porto).

SEAT BELTS: Use of seat belts is mandatory in Portugal outside the cities and towns and the law is enforced, so get into the habit of buckling up when you get into the car. Outside the cities, the Guarda Nacional Republicana, a national police force, is in charge of traffic. They conduct spot checks constantly around the country, pulling over cars (using criteria known only to them) and checking for valid documents. Be sure to carry your car papers at all times.

TOLL ROADS: There are almost no toll roads in Portugal. The short stretches of freeway (AUTO ESTRADA) around Lisbon and Porto charge tolls, but their length makes the cost minor. The 25th of April Bridge across the Tagus at Lisbon also charges a small toll.

TRAFFIC: On smaller roads it can be ferocious. A particular danger is the large number of pedestrians sharing the roadways, even at night, when few roads are illuminated. We suggest that you try to drive as little as possible at night. Local drivers are not known for their caution. In the large cities, unfamiliarity combined with traffic, parking problems and the fact that almost no two streets are parallel make driving a trial for all but the bravest of souls. Our preference and advice is to leave the car in the hotel parking lot (or one recommended by the hotel) and take cabs or walk around the large cities. Taxis are plentiful and very reasonable. In downtown Lisbon you might try the subway system (called the Metro and marked with signs bearing a large "M"). If you are stopping to visit a town along an itinerary route, we suggest you park on or near a main square (for easy recall), then venture by foot into those streets that were never designed with cars in mind.

Traffic regulations are similar to most other countries. Driving is on the right-hand side of the road, passing on the left. At intersections of roughly equal roads, and in roundabouts, vehicles on the right have the right-of-way unless otherwise indicated.

ROAD SIGNS: The method of indicating where a road is going is slightly different from the U.S. standard. Usually (unfortunately, not always) the next town of any size is indicated along with either the next large town or the last town on the road in question. The road number is almost never on a sign, but is usually found on concrete markers that indicate each kilometer along the road. However they are sometimes missing, upended or simply unreadable at normal speeds. All this calls for some care when following a map through unfamiliar territory.

Before setting out, prepare yourself by learning the international road signs so that you can obey all the rules of the road and avoid the embarrassment of heading the wrong way down a small street or parking in a forbidden area. There are several basic sign shapes. The triangular signs warn that there is danger ahead. The circular signs indicate compulsory rules and information. The square signs give information concerning telephones, parking, camping, etc.

ECONOMY

Portugal has long been known as a travel bargain, although it has now been admitted to the European Common Market and most observers think that prices will rise to near the level of the other members during 1986-87. The socialist revolution in 1974 caused tourism to grind to a virtual halt for about four years. Since then, a more moderate government has sought to revitalize the industry, but progress is slow due to a generally weak economy, and first-rate accommodation is still lacking in some parts of the country.

ENGLISH

English-speaking tourists account for as much as 40% of the total in some areas. In the large hotels in the major cities, you won't even need to use your phrase book (we suggest the Berlitz European Phrase Book). And, in the pousadas and elsewhere, you'll usually find that someone speaks enough English to ease your way through check-in to check-out. If not, just pull out your trusty phrase book and point - the Portuguese are friendly and you'll eventually make yourself understood (and probably learn some Portuguese while you're at it). If you make advance reservations, be sure to take your letters of confirmation with you; it will save a lot of pointing.

FESTIVALS AND FOLKLORE

The major national holidays are April 25 (1974 Revolution), May 1 (Day of the Worker), June 10 (death of the great poet, Camoes), October 5 (Establishment of the Republic) and December 1 (Independence from Spain, 1640). Of course, Christmas, New Year's Day and Easter are also major observances.

In addition, every Portuguese town has its patron saint, and every saint its day of honor, so there are as many festivals as there are Portuguese towns. If you know where you want to go ahead of time, write the Portuguese National Tourist Office for a list of festival dates so that you might arrange your visit to coincide with one or several of these colorful local events. (Be forewarned, however, that hotel space can be a problem during festival time.)

Each week in most towns there is a major market day (feira, or fair) which is held in one of the main squares. We have mentioned a number of these in the itinerary section. You should try to visit these to see a wider selection of folk art and handicrafts (and at better prices) than you will find in the shops.

All over Portugal, from April to October, major festivals will often include the unique local variant of bullfighting.   Unlike the Spanish version, in Portugal the bull is not killed (although he is surely greatly annoyed by the whole operation), and part of the show features an amazing performance by the bullfighter on horseback.   If you've been put off by the more commonly known Spanish version of the spectacle, the Portuguese twist might be an acceptable alternative.

The archetypical musical form in Portugal is the FADO, normally a mournful lament on the fateful adversity of life.   It is usually sung by a female accompanied by one or more 12-string guitars.   The Coimbra style is characterized by a happier, sometimes satirical tone.   Performances are most common in Lisbon cafes and clubs and, to a lesser extent, in other cities.   They are often included on city tours, if you prefer that approach.

FOOD AND DRINK

The government rates restaurants from one to four crossed forks and spoons (four is best); however its rating system is based on such matters as the number of choices on the menu, the wine cellar, or whether the menu is translated, rather than the quality of the food, so it can be misleading. A modest-appearing and reasonably priced restaurant will often offer good, regional fare. Servings tend to be quite generous.

Not surprisingly, given its physical proximity to (and its economic dependence upon) the sea, the Portuguese menu features an incredibly wide variety of seafood. Many of these are totally unknown to Americans (even where the menu is translated, it doesn't necessarily help). Items such as ENGUIAS (baby eels) and numerous shellfish are best viewed as an adventure. You will find many of them excellent and should definitely experiment. By far the most common single item on the menu is BACALHAU (cod). This is often dried, salted cod which is soaked to restore the softness and cooked mixed with other items such as eggs and potatoes -- there must be as many different recipes as there are chefs.

Pork and lamb are the most prevalent meat entries on a menu. You'll find that vegetables accompany the main course with somewhat more frequency than in other European countries.

Wine is ubiquitous. In the large, fancy restaurants a good selection of imported wines is usually available in addition to the extensive native listing. In smaller ones the options are mostly Portuguese, which is often a rich selection indeed, and fun to sample. We found ourselves returning repeatedly to the very smooth reds from the COLARES region, but almost every area has some good local wine which is quite economical. You'll seldom be disappointed with the VINHO DA REGIAO (regional wine) in any decent restaurant. Unlike most countries where wine comes in three varieties - TINTO (red), BRANCO (white) and ROSADO (rose) - in Portugal there is also VINHO VERDE (green). The last is a young wine grown in the north and actually comes in both red and white versions (not really green), although the white is much more common. It is a light wine and has a slight sparkle.

Portugal's most famous drink is, of course, PORTO, the well-known fortified wine from the Upper-Douro-River territory which is made in the city of the same name. It comes in seemingly endless varieties from vintage (single good year) to blended (several years mixed), and from deep red and sweet (usually for dessert) to white and dry (for an aperitif).

CERVEJA (beer) is another favorite liquid refreshment, and is always good, sometimes excellent, especially on hot days in a shady outdoor cafe. SAGRES is the most common local variety, but imported beers are also widely available (at a higher price, of course).

Another customary beverage ordered in Portuguese restaurants is, believe it or not, water: the bottled kind. Though there is nothing wrong with AGUA DA TORNEIRA (tap water), AGUA MINERAL (mineral water) is popular in either LITRO or MEIO LITRO (liter or half-liter) sizes. It may also be ordered COM (with) or SEM (without) GAS (carbonation). You'll notice that the Portuguese often dilute their wine with it.

Once you leave the large cities and tourist-frequented restaurants, you'll find that menus are often poorly (and sometimes amusingly) translated, or not translated at all. The following list includes some of the terms of traditional specialties to be found on most Portuguese menus:

PEQUENO ALMOCO - (breakfast) - This is always a Continental breakfast in Portugal, consisting of PAO (bread) and/or PAO DOCE (sweet rolls) along with CAFE (coffee), CHA (tea), LEITE (milk) or CHOCOLATE (hot chocolate). Hotels in Portugal are required by law to provide breakfast and to include it in their quoted prices. The larger hotels will often offer other items at an extra charge such as OVOS (eggs), which may be ordered MEXIDOS (scrambled), MAL PASADOS or QUENTES (soft-boiled), ESCALFADOS (poached), FRITOS (fried) or COZIDOS (hard-boiled).

ALMOCO - (lunch) - This is usually taken between 12:30 and 1:30 p.m. It normally consists of several courses: ACEPIPES (appetizers), SOPAS (soup, usually of the thick variety), CARNE (meat dishes), PEIXE E MARISCOS (fish and shellfish), SOBREMESA (desserts) and, of course, VINHO. No one orders all these courses - two or three is most common. Restaurants will usually offer an a la carte EMENTA (menu) and a smaller MENU (daily special-price meal). The latter will have fewer choices and frequently two prices - one includes soup, one main course and dessert, the other adds another main course. This menu is almost always a relative bargain if you like its selections.

CHA - (tea) - This follows the British tradition of tea accompanied by various pastries and is to be found in numerous CASAS DE CHA (tea houses), especially in the larger cities. The Portuguese, of course, were the first to import tea from the Orient in any appreciable amount. The word CHA comes from the Chinese word for it, while the word tea, used in most Western languages, comes from the Chinese word for leaf.

JANTAR - (dinner) - This meal is taken around 8:00 p.m. and usually consists of the same combinations mentioned above under ALMOCO.

ACORDA - This is a thick soup with various bases (one of which is almost always garlic) and is served with bread in it.

AZEITE - (olive oil) - About the only kind of oil used to cook with in Portugal and used in many, many dishes.

CATAPLANA - This actually refers to the utensil - a flat frying pan with a curved bottom and a hinged lid, usually of tin or copper. It is frequently used over an open fire to cook mixtures of seafood (clams, shrimp, etc.) and other meats and sausage. One southern specialty is AMEIJOAS (clams) A CATAPLANA. This is another dish which varies considerably from one place to another and is a national favorite.

CALDEIRADA - A hearty fish chowder.

CALDO VERDE - A potato and cabbage or kale soup.   It's on almost every menu.

CARNE (meat) - ANHO (lamb), VITELA (veal), BIFE (beefsteak), CABRITO (kid), PORCO (pork), LEITAO (suckling pig), FRANGO (chicken) are all widespread.   COSTELETA is a chop and LOMBO is a filet.   Several of these items are also used commonly in stew (GUISADO).   They may be ASSADO (roasted), GRELHADO (grilled), NAS BRASAS (charcoal grilled) or SALTEADO (sauteed).

PEIXE E MARISCOS - (fish and shellfish) - AMEIJOAS (clams), ATUM (tuna), BACALHAU (cod), CAMAROES (shrimp), ESPADARTE (swordfish), PEIXE ESPADA (scabbard fish), LINGUADO (sole), LAGOSTA (crayfish), LAVAGANTE (lobster), PREGADO (turbot), PESCADA (hake), TRUTA (trout) and SALMAO (salmon) number among many others on a menu.   LULA (squid) and CHOCOS (cuttlefish) are also frequent.   In the north you will find LAMPREIA (lamprey) to be common.

LEGUMES E HORTALICAS (vegetables) - ALCACHOFRA (artichoke), ALFACE (lettuce), ARROZ (rice), BATATA (potato), CEBOLHA (onion), CENOURA (carrot), ESPARGOS (asparagus), COGUMELOS (mushrooms), ESPINAFRE (spinach), GRELOS (turnip greens) are some constant ones.

SALADA MISTA - (tossed green salad) - Besides lettuce, this usually contains any or all of the following: olive, tomato, onion and raw vegetables.   But remember that there is usually only one salad dressing: VINAGRE (vinegar) and AZEITE (olive oil).

Recurrent condiments are ALHO (garlic), COENTROS (coriander) and PIRI-PIRI (a spicy, chili sauce).

Fruits, such as AMEIXAS (plums), FIGOS (figs), PERAS (pears), MACAS (apples) and MORANGOS (strawberries) are popular desserts.   Every region has its particular variety of a confection based on sweetened egg yolks which has as many names as versions.

GEOGRAPHY
_____

The land area of Portugal is about 36,000 square miles, or about the size of Indiana.   It is generally a rectangle of about 350 miles long by 100 miles wide. It is bordered on the north and east by Spain (with about 800 miles of common border) and on the south and west by the Atlantic Ocean.   The northern half of the country is studded with low mountain ranges, with only the Serra da Estrela approaching imposing dimensions (its highest peak, Torre, rises to 6,500 feet). The southern half is characterized by plains with less frequent mountain outcroppings.   The Serra de Monchique divides the southern tip from the rest of the country and shelters the famous Algarve from the cooler climatic tendencies of the north. Portugal's population is about 10 million. That translates to about 277 inhabitants per square mile, similar to Ohio or Pennsylvania.

GOVERNMENT

The national government is a parliamentary system similar to that of France, with both a President (five-year term) and a Prime Minister (elected every four years). The Revolution of 1974 and the resulting constitution of 1976 instituted an essentially socialist government resulting in a great deal of nationalization. Subsequent modifications have tended to reverse that trend somewhat and to narrow the powers of the Armed Forces, who had carried out the revolution. Other moderations followed, although the current constitution still calls for movement toward a classless society.

HISTORY

EARLY PERIOD: Traces of cave-dwelling prehistoric man - Neolithic, Megalithic and Magdalenian - have been discovered all over the Peninsula. Around the 6th century B.C., the area was widely inhabited by the Celts from the north, the Iberians from Africa, and the warrior Lusitanians who inhabited the area between the Tagus and the Douro Rivers. The Phoenicians, the Greeks, and especially the Carthaginians, founded ports along the coast. As a result of the Second Punic War (2nd century B.C.), the Peninsula became a Roman colony.

ROMAN PERIOD: Hispania was the most heavily colonized of all Rome's dominions and their 600-year presence is the wellspring for modern Portuguese culture - its language, legal system and religion. The Portuguese pride themselves on the fact that the Lusitanians, under their leader Viriato, resisted

Roman domination longer than any other people (he was finally assassinated by the Romans in 139 B.C., and is now considered a national hero). When the entire Roman Empire was overrun by the Germanic tribes from the north, Portugal was to suffer the same fate.

VISIGOTH PERIOD: By the 5th century A.D. the Visigoths had subdued the Peninsula almost completely (the Basque area of Spain was an exception), and had adopted Roman Catholicism as their own. As kingdoms were combined and divided over the next centuries, their feudalistic system presaged the traditional Portuguese regions. Their political structure, involving a monarch who served at the pleasure of the feudal lords, was subject to considerable instability as the kaleidoscope of dynastic unions changed constantly. This characteristic strife provided the opportunity, in 711, for the Moors (Islamic Africans) to invade and sweep across the Peninsula from south to north in the space of two decades.

MOORISH PERIOD: The Moors were a tolerant people and allowed a diversity of religions to coexist. At that point in history they represented the highest level of civilization in the West and exerted influence on the development of Portuguese culture, especially in the southern part of the country. By the 10th century the Emirate of Cordoba, which included present-day Portugal, was perhaps the most advanced area in Europe. Nevertheless, the Christians regrouped in the inaccessible mountains of Asturias to launch a crusade to reconquer their territory from the Moslems lasting almost eight centuries.

RECONQUEST PERIOD: Legend has it that a Christian leader Pelayo, set up the Kingdom of Asturias after the defeat of the Moors at Covadonga in 718. The Christians established their capital at Leon in 914.   Under their control were Asturias, Galicia and part of Burgos.   They discovered the remains of St. James the Apostle in Galicia, and he became the patron saint of the Reconquest.

By 1095 the northern part of Portugal was held by the Christians, and King Alfonso VI of Castile and Leon created the separate county of Portucalia (named for Portus Cale, the modern city of Porto) and granted it to Count Henry of Burgundy.   In 1139 Henry's son, Afonso Henriques, assumed the title of Afonso I and proclaimed independence from Castile and Leon.   Struggles with the Moors consumed the next 100 years, with the Algarve finally falling to the Christians in 1250.   The stage was thus set for the definitive establishment of the modern Portuguese nation.

MODERN PERIOD: The first monarch to move substantially in that direction was the esteemed King Dom Dinis (reign: 1279-1325), called "O Lavrador" (the Farmer).   He is credited with developing the agricultural economy of the country and securing its territory from the aggressive, emerging nation next door.   (Not yet known as Spain, the kingdoms of Castile and Leon controlled almost all of the border with Portugal and were pretty much equivalent to it in size.)   When not distracted with stimulating farming, and establishing and fortifying towns (which may still be found atop hills along the Spanish border), Dom Dinis was fascinated by Portugal's only other neighbor, the Atlantic Ocean. He strengthened the country's merchant marine fleet and sought out the most capable European navigators to teach in Portugal.   It's believed that early Atlantic expeditions resulted in the discovery of the Azores during this period. Thus King Dinis initiated what was to culminate in Portugal's finest hour in the 15th and 16th centuries.

In 1385 King Joao I finally defeated the Castilians in a decisive battle at Aljubarrota, consolidating the country's independence for the next two centuries, and allowing full attention to be given to conquering the sea. His youngest son, Prince Henry, established a school of navigation at Sagres on the southwestern tip of Portugal in 1418 and expansion activity began in earnest. He became known to history as Henry the Navigator, and though he never went on the voyages himself, he was obsessively dedicated to organizing them.

Portuguese sailors and navigators began a series of voyages down the coast of Africa, each expedition pushing the frontier farther south. Economic motivation was strong, since dwindling European gold supplies were being poured into the thriving spice trade through middle men of the Middle East and Venice. Portugal was hemmed in by Spain, so Africa, and later the Orient, provided the only direction for expansion.

In 1482 an expedition reached the mouth of the River Congo, and six years later Bartolomeu Dias sailed far enough around the Cape of Good Hope to realize that he was probably in the Indian Ocean. The king at the time was Joao II, arguably Portugal's greatest monarch and styled "The Perfect Prince," although it was he who turned away Columbus before the Spanish Queen Isabella took up his offer. Joao II was a vigorous supporter of these enterprises, but apparently believed his own navigators when they opined that Columbus's proposed route to the Orient was impractical. In 1494 (after Columbus's discovery of the New World) Joao II negotiated the Treaty of Tordesillas which divided the world between Spain and Portugal for exploration and colonization. Portugal got everything east of the line approximately following the 50' W line of longitude and Spain everything to the west.

Under King Manuel I, who succeeded Joao II in 1495, Vasco da Gama finally reached India in 1498. Manuel I built the incredible Hieronymite monastery in Belem, near Lisbon, to commemorate the event. The Portuguese then attained Newfoundland, Greenland, Labrador and, in 1500, Brazil. By 1513 they had sailed to China and Timor in the Orient, then proceeded to Japan a few years later. Portugal's empire, unlike Spain's, was based primarily on maritime trade, and the eastern "colonies" were simply trading enclaves. While they sparked a lot of activity, they were apparently not that profitable, with what profit there was going primarily to the crown rather than creating an entrepreneurial class.

By 1580, when King Sebastiao attempted a crusading expedition to Morocco and disappeared, the Portuguese were in no shape to resist the pretensions of Sebastiao's uncle, Phillip II of Spain, to the throne. Thus began the long-dreaded "Spanish Captivity" of 60 years. During this period Portugal began to lose its empire one piece at a time, mostly to the Dutch. At the same time, Lisbon became the third-largest city in Europe, surpassed only by Paris and Naples in population. When a subsequent Spanish Phillip increased Portugal's taxes to help finance Spain's 30-Years War with France, it proved to be the last straw. In 1640 the Spanish were overthrown and the Duke of Braganca assumed the throne as Joao IV. The remainder of the century was mostly dedicated to restoring Portugal's devastated economy.

Toward the end of the 17th century gold was discovered in Brazil, and a new era of prosperity followed for the Portuguese monarchs. The flow of the precious metal (soon to be accompanied by diamonds) increased throughout the first half of the 18th century, but since it was used to finance imports, the nation's internal economy derived little benefit. It was during this period that the art of working gold reached its zenith, as can be seen in various museums and cathedral treasuries throughout the country. The revenue from Brazil also allowed Joao V (1706-1750) to construct the giant palace monastery at Mafra. By the time he died in 1750 Portugal had regained some of its former importance in Europe.

His son and successor was Jose I, one of those monarchs, like Louis XIII in France, about whom you never hear because they were eclipsed by the power and achievements of their ministers. In Louis' case it was Cardinal Richelieu and in

Jose's it was the Marques de Pombal, Sebastiao Jose de Carvalho e Melo. Pombal was, in the style of the mid-18th century, a product of the Enlightenment and a believer in the notion that the best ruler was the enlightened despot. The King was a product of the lavish court and a believer in things more pleasurable than the dreary job of governing. They were made for each other. Then, on November 1, 1755, a tremendous earthquake destroyed most of Lisbon and caused severe damage to other cities in the region. In the ensuing chaos Pombal seems to have kept his head and consolidated his power, which he wielded for the next 22 years. Most of his administration seems to have been marked by failure, although he was often in the European limelight. He was anticlerical to the extreme of expelling the Jesuits entirely. He attempted to establish state monopolies in various economic sectors, but there is little evidence that they made much economic sense. He did rationalize much of the administration of Brazil (his legacy there is as an important, progressive figure). When Jose died in 1777, his successor Maria I relieved Pombal of his duties and he retired to his estates in the town that bears his name.

In 1807 Napoleon's forces entered Portugal and marched toward Lisbon. The Prince Regent Joao (later King Joao VI) accepted British advice and hastily moved the court to Brazil, where it remained for 14 years to govern the still-vast Portuguese Empire. The Portuguese who remained behind wasted no time in striking back at the French. An agreement was negotiated with England (no friend of Napoleon), and a combined force of British and Portuguese armies headed by the Duke of Wellington soon drove the French back across the Spanish border.

The 19th century in Portugal was witness mostly to struggles between the constitutionalists' desire to end absolutism and their royalist opponents. Joao VI had made Brazil a kingdom in its own right and left his son, Pedro IV, to rule. Two years later Pedro proclaimed independence for that immense and wealthy colony (naming himself Emperor), and Portugal was powerless to hold on to it. On Joao's death in 1826, Pedro was theoretically both Emperor of Brazil and

King of Portugal. Since that was not possible, he attempted to install his daughter Maria on the Portuguese throne. There followed an eight-year battle between the forces of Pedro's brother Miguel and those loyal to Pedro's daughter Maria. Pedro himself was forced to abdicate his Brazilian throne in favor of his son, so returned to Europe to support the claims of his daughter. He managed to defeat his brother and banish him into exile. Maria II was then crowned queen at the age of 15. Her faction was in favor of a constitution and it was duly pronounced the same year.

Having been through 25 years of strife, Portugal now found itself saddled with a huge debt, without its main source of income (Brazil) and with two contentious factions promoting different constitutions. On a liberal move, all religious orders were abolished and their property confiscated. (This is why, as you will see in the hotel descriptions, many former monasteries are now government property and some are pousadas.) The rest of the century saw numerous small-scale revolts and a struggle to match the pace of economic development being experienced in the rest of the continent, while also defending the remaining overseas possessions from encroachment by other European powers. Failure to do all this was a major determinant in the revolt of October 5, 1910, which overthrew the monarch (Manuel II) and established the Republic - the third in Europe (after Switzerland and France).

The next 15 years brought over 40 changes of government by various means, mostly coups. Portugal entered World War I on the Allied side and fought in Africa and Europe. In 1928 Antonio Oliveira Salazar, the Finance Minister, was charged with rebuilding the national economy. Due to his success, he was named Prime Minister in 1932 and arranged the promulgation of a new constitution which created the "New State," a kind of corporative Republic. Salazar liked his job and remained as Prime Minister for the next 36 years. The regime was primarily authoritarian, with control maintained by repression and sometimes brutality. Though not generally considered as bad as Generalissimo Franco's contemporaneous regime in neighboring Spain, it was essentially a dictatorship. Portugal remained neutral during World War II, but was commonly perceived as sympathetic to its old British allies. Lisbon became a rendezvous spot for spies from both sides, as spy-novel fans will undoubtedly recall.

After World War II it was Salazar's primitive economic theories which prevented development in national industry, even though conditions conducive to an industrial boom existed, since Portugal had made a tidy profit selling tungsten from its colonies to both sides during the war.

By the 1960s Portugal's control over its so-called "Overseas Provinces" began to weaken. India reclaimed Goa and national liberation movements developed in Angola and Mozambique. During the entire decade Portugal was being drained of both money and young men as the wars continued. The inability or unwillingness of the Salazar regime to move toward decolonization fueled the fires of resentment among even those elements of society - the peasants, the Armed Forces - who might have been his staunchest supporters. As more and more families lost sons in faraway lands, and pressure mounted on the Armed Forces to save the colonies, the regime lost support. The officers' corps was increasingly being recruited from the lower middle class as the elite refused to serve for the first time. This changed the social and political outlook of the Armed Forces. In 1968 Salazar was forced to step down by ill health and his personal popularity as a stabilizing figure was lost to his successors. A few liberalizing gestures proved insufficient to quell unrest and, finally, on April 25, 1974, a radical military group carried out an almost bloodless coup (popularized by the famous posters of soldiers with flowers in the ends of their rifles, thus styling the movement the "Carnation Revolution"). Within a few months the colonies were liberated and the country braced for the return of over half a million refugees to their homeland on the continent.

The original architects of the revolution were mostly communist-oriented elements of the Armed Forces who had joined in an organization called the

Armed Forces Movement (MFA). The MFA set up a junta to run the government until elections could be held. The more moderate socialist party was in disarray and unable to mount opposition to the extremists. Within less than a year some 60% of the economy had been nationalized and several million acres of farmland had been collectivized. Even small businesses were summarily seized in dramatic fashion. THE GUARDIAN reported that at a country club in the Algarve which had been requisitioned by the army, a sign was mounted proclaiming it open to "anyone except members."

Elections for a constitutional convention were finally set for April 25, 1975, the anniversary of the coup. The MFA had not constituted itself as a political party and presented no candidates. The socialist party's strong showing indicated a clear preference for an evolutionary rather than revolutionary approach. The MFA junta continued to move to the left, in contrast to the will of the people. Opposition to the leaders of MFA grew, both within and outside the military. By the close of 1975 Portugal seemed again on the brink of a civil war. Fortunately, the MFA saw the writing on the wall and capitulated, avoiding otherwise inevitable bloodshed.

The revolution ended and a period of leftist socialism under a very radical, though democratic, constitution was ushered in. The economy was in chaos resulting from the rash behavior of the MFA. Subsequent governments have addressed this problem and have backed off many of the radical policies of the revolution in favor of a more moderate approach. On January 1, 1986, Portugal achieved full status in the European Economic Community. The Portuguese hope this move will help bring its economy up to the level of the rest of Europe.

HOTEL DESCRIPTIONS

This guide is divided into two sections, with hotel descriptions in each. The first section guides you through Portugal on researched itineraries, pointing out the most interesting sights along the way, and suggesting a hotel for each destination. The other section is a complete list of hotels with more detailed descriptions ordered alphabetically by town. The list provides a wide selection of hotels throughout Portugal. A description, an illustration and pertinent information is provided on each one. Some are posh, offering every amenity and a price to match; others small and cozy (often with correspondingly smaller prices), providing only the important amenities such as private baths, personality and gracious personnel. Occasionally, a perfect choice doesn't exist in a place which really must be visited, in which case we have recommended the best available.

For some of you, cost will not be a factor; for others, it will be a necessary consideration. We are happy to report, however, that you still get a lot of value for your dollar in Portugal, and that there are some wonderful hotels in the inexpensive-to-moderate range. We have been to every hotel which appears in the book, and have included none without special appeal, no matter what the price. What we have tried to do is to indicate what each hotel has to offer and to describe the setting, so that you can make the choice to suit your own preferences and holiday. We feel that if you know what to expect, you won't be disappointed, so we have tried to be candid and honest in our appraisals.

HOTEL RATES AND INFORMATION

The rates hotels charge are no longer regulated by the Portuguese government, but owners do have to register their rates with the government each year and cannot change them until the next year. Inflation causes yearly upward adjustments in prices and, if we were to quote them, they would be outdated by the time this book is in your hands. To further complicate matters, most hotels have an intricate system of rates, which will vary according to season, local special events, and additional features such as sitting rooms, balconies and views. What we have tried to do is to give a relative comparison of the same type of room for each hotel.   Prices are based on a double room with private bath and breakfast for two people during the summer (high) season.   And, since relative prices seldom change - an "inexpensive" hotel will remain so relative to a "luxury" hotel (except that they will both be a bit more expensive next year) - we have chosen to categorize hotel price ranges in the Hotel Section instead of giving exact prices.

Budget - Under $30

Inexpensive - $30 to $45

Moderate - $46 to $60

Expensive - $61 to $80

Very Expensive - Over $80

Hotels are required to provide a Continental breakfast and include it in the basic room price.   Many hotels also have a rate for "pensao completa," which means breakfast and two meals, or "meia pensao," which is usually breakfast and one other meal (called American Plan and Modified American Plan respectively in English).   These can constitute good value and should be investigated where convenient.   They often require a minimum stay of about three days.

HOTEL RESERVATIONS

Whether or not to reserve ahead is not a question with a simple answer; it depends upon the flexibility in your timetable and in your temperament.   It also depends to a large extent on the season in which you are travelling.   For example, during the peak season of June through August, accommodation at the Pousada do Castelo in Obidos normally requires reservations months in advance.   Other popular hotels with limited rooms are similarly booked. And careful tourists make arrangements months in advance to secure desirable accommodations during a local festival. On the other hand, throughout much of the year space can be obtained in most places with one day's notice, or less. If you have your heart set on a particular inn, you should certainly make a reservation. But, though comforting, reservations can be confining since you have to plan your travels in advance. It comes down to a choice between the security of knowing where you will be each night and the adventure of being able to tarry longer in that "extra special" place you find on your journey.

Advance reservations call for some homework before you go and limit your flexibility once you arrive, but they will ensure that you get to experience those special places Portugal has to offer. For those who prefer security (and who are going in the summer months) there are several ways of making reservations which we have listed below.

TRAVEL AGENT: A travel agent can be of great assistance - particularly if your own time is valuable. A knowledgeable agent can handle all the details of your holiday and "tie" it all together for you in package form, including hotel reservations, airline tickets, boat tickets, train reservations, etc. There should be no charge for your airline tickets, but most travel agencies charge for their other services. Our advice is to be frank about how much you want to spend, and ask exactly what your agent can do for you and what the charges will be. If he's not familiar with every place in this guide, lend it to him - it is written as a guide for travel agents as well as vacationers.

LETTER: If you start early, you can write to the hotels directly for your reservations. Be brief in your request. Clearly state the following: number of people in your party; how many and what size rooms you require; date of arrival and date of departure; ask rate per night and deposit needed. When you receive a reply, send the deposit requested (if any) and ask for confirmation of receipt. Note: when corresponding with Portugal be sure to spell out the month since, in

Europe, they reverse our system - 7/8 means the 7th of August, not the 8th of July.   Since the mail to Portugal tends to be slow, especially outside the large cities, you should allow six weeks for a reply.   Although most hotels can find someone able to understand a letter in English, on page 205 (just behind the hotel listings) we have provided a reservation-request letter written in Portuguese with an English translation.   Following this format you can tailor a letter in Portuguese to meet your requirements.   The translation includes phrases which will enable you to request specific features, such as sea view, balcony and suite. Check the hotel's description for recommendations in this regard before writing.

TELEPHONE: Another method of making reservations is to call.   The cost is minimal if you dial direct on a weekend (business days for hotels), and the advantage great since you can have your answer immediately (though you should still request written confirmation).   If space is not available, you can look right away for an alternative.   Remember that Portugal is five hours later than New York for most of the year and time your call accordingly.   Basically, the system is to dial the international access code (011), then the country code for Portugal (351) and the city code and telephone number listed in the hotel descriptions. Don't worry that phone numbers have different numbers of digits - that's the way it works in Portugal.

TELEX: If you have access to a telex machine, this is another efficient way to reach a hotel.   When a hotel has a telex we have included the number in the description section.   Again, be sure to specify your arrival and departure dates, number in your party and what type of room you want.   And, of course, include your telex number for their response.

U.S. REPRESENTATIVE: A few of the hotels we've recommended and all of the pousadas have a U.S. representative through which reservations can be made. This can be an extremely convenient and efficient way to secure reservations. The service is not free, though it is not expensive.   However, if you plan to stay in several pousadas, one well-thought-out phone call to their representative could finalize a large part of your holiday. When hotels have U.S. representatives, their name and telephone numbers are listed in the hotel section.

INFORMATION

A rich source for free information about Portugal is the Portuguese National Tourist Office, 548 Fifth Ave., New York, NY 10036. They can provide you with general information about the country or, at your request, specific information about towns, regions and festivals. Also, if you send a request for information addressed to the Posto de Turismo (Tourism Office) of almost any town in Portugal, you will be inundated with colorful and informative brochures. The tourist offices throughout the country are usually prominently located, and offer an incomparable on-site resource, furnishing town maps and details on local and regional highlights. They are frequently open seven days a week and their hours are usually longer than most other establishments. They are identified by the sign "Turismo" and someone usually speaks English. Baedeker's PORTUGAL and the Michelin "Green Guide" for Portugal are excellent sources for more detail on sights, museums and places of interest.

ITINERARIES

The first section of this guide features itineraries covering much of Portugal. They may be taken in whole or in part, or tied together for a longer journey. Each of the itineraries highlights a different region of the country, and they are of different lengths, enabling you to find one or more to suit your individual taste and schedule. They are designed to accommodate customization.

We have intentionally not specified how many nights to stay at each destination. Your personality and time restraints will dictate what is best for you. Some travellers wish to squeeze as much as possible into their allotted vacation time, even if it means rising with the sun and never settling more than one night in any destination. Others, ourselves included, prefer to concentrate their time in fewer locations in order to relax, unpack and savor the atmosphere and novelty of the spot. If you're new to Portugal and planning a trip there, we hope that, upon reading through the itineraries and hotel descriptions, you'll get a feel for which places merit the most time and which can be done justice with an overnight stay. In other words, this guide should be a reference and not a prescription for your personalized trip.

Keep in mind that the hotels recommended in the itineraries represent only about half of those described in this guide. There are alternate choices in the hotel listings, which are also indicated by stars on the itinerary maps so, if your first choice is booked, or you're wandering off the itineraries, other recommended hotels are to be found throughout the country.

MAPS
———

Accompanying each itinerary is a map showing the routing and places of interest along the way. These are artist's renderings and are not meant to replace a good commercial map. Before departure, you should procure a detailed map with highway numbers, expressways, alternate routes and kilometrage. There is a Michelin red series (1:1,000,000) map of all of Spain and Portugal and a regional (yellow series, 1:400,000) map of just Portugal.

If you live in an area where it is difficult to locate reference materials, we recommend The Complete Traveler as an excellent and reliable source. If you call or contact them by mail, they will send you a catalog of maps and books, and can often accommodate special requests or items not advertised on their list. Their address is: The Complete Traveler, 199 Madison Ave., New York, NY 10016, (212) 685-9000.

Between the itinerary section and the hotel listing, you'll find a map showing all the towns in which hotels are recommended. Each town is marked with a number, and the numbers flow geographically across the map. The numbers will help you locate the nearest recommended hotel to your chosen destination (or nearby alternates should your first choice be unavailable). These map numbers are cross-referenced in the hotel listing and the index. Each time a hotel is mentioned the map number is provided.

POUSADAS AND ESTALAGENS

The Portuguese government operates a system of hotels called "Pousadas" (literally "stopping place" or, more commonly, "inn") which are widely acknowledged to constitute the most outstanding bargain in the country. The first inns were created in the 1940s in an effort to encourage tourism to those areas lacking proper hotel facilities. New ones have been added periodically ever since, the latest being the Pousada de Santa Marinha in Guimaraes, which opened in 1985. In the few areas where they compete with existing hotels, they attempt to raise the standards of professionalism by having well-trained staffs and up-to-date physical facilities. They will almost never be the least expensive accommodations available, but you can count on getting your "escudo's worth." Many are installed in remodelled historic buildings, while others are modern constructions built in regional style. While each is unique, the standard of service and quality of accommodation are consistently high. Another bonus is that there are almost always signs which lead you from the edge of the town to the pousada by the most efficient route. This may seem minor, but it can be a real time-saver. All have good to excellent dining rooms with regional culinary specialties and often provide good places for lunch if you are on the road. We will mention the pousadas which are en route between itinerary stops for this reason. We have not eaten in all the pousadas mentioned but, after having sampled the fare in many, we feel confident in recommending them.

While you could travel throughout Portugal staying in nothing but pousadas and be assured of exceptional lodging, we also recommend many other hotels which merit consideration. It is also the case that the entire system is being remodelled over a period of time and some pousadas will be closed in any given period. You can check on closures and receive illustrated information about the government chain by writing to the Portuguese National Tourist Office. The system is also constantly expanding so it may be useful to know where the new ones are. Throughout the hotel descriptions the abbreviation Pda. before the hotel name indicates which are pousadas.

Estalagens are privately owned inns which are supposed to maintain similar standards to the pousadas, which many do. They also usually have signs leading you to them. Our experience indicates, however, that there is more variation in quality than is the case with pousadas. Some are modern, rather lackluster establishments, but we discovered some charming examples and have included them in the hotel descriptions.

SECURITY WHILE TRAVELLING

Most Portuguese are friendly and gracious. They are helpful and open to tourists. You will generally feel welcome in their country. As in any other country, however, there are a few people who see tourists as targets for crime. The problems are basically purse-snatching and breaking into cars and are by and large limited to the larger cities. There is no reason to believe the problem is any greater than in large U.S. cities. The answer is caution and common sense. Especially in crowded areas, be cautious with your wallet or purse. Don't leave anything in your car, ever. Lock your valuables in the hotel safe. Carry traveller's checks rather than large amounts of cash. Take the same precautions you would at home to avoid any unfortunate incidents.

SHOPPING

The most popular items to buy in Portugal are ceramics (both decorative and functional) which vary extensively from region to region. The porcelain works at Vista Alegre (near Aveiro) are world-famous. Lace and woolen goods abound, and are well-made and reasonable. Port wine is not worth lugging home because the best brands can probably be found in your local liquor store at similar prices. A few specialty items are worth investigating in certain areas and they will be noted in the itineraries.

TELEPHONES

It is quite a bit more expensive to call home from Portugal than vice versa but, if you want to call home, the most economical method is to search out the local post office, where you simply give the operator the phone number, after which he will place the call, indicate the booth for you to take it in once it's placed, and tell you the charges afterward. Some hotels have direct-dial phones for long distance, but most of the smaller ones do not.

TIME

You will find the typical Portuguese schedule easy to adjust to. Breakfast is at the same time as at home. Restaurants start serving the midday meal around 1:00 p.m. and dinner is typically served from 8:00 p.m. on.

Shops usually close from 12:30 or 1:00 p.m. until 3:30 or 4:00 p.m., when they reopen until 6:00 (except on Saturdays). Most cathedrals do the same, as do the smaller museums; the larger ones often stay open all day. Monday is the most common day for museum closures.

TIPPING

As everywhere,' tipping is not clearcut. Most restaurants and hotels include "servicio" in the bill but, in restaurants, a small tip is expected anyway when the service is good. Small means different things to different people but certainly should not exceed 10% and probably should be more like 5%. In other situations tips probably should average about half what you might tip at home.

TRAINS

The Portuguese National Rail System (called CP) has a somewhat sketchy network of trains. Service is, of course, more frequent between and around the major cities. There are several discount schemes available. If you don't plan to travel by car, but do plan to travel extensively, consider the Eurail Pass, which must be purchased before leaving home, and affords unlimited train travel all over Europe without additional charge. The Portuguese National Railway is represented in the United States by the French National Railroads, 610 Fifth Ave., New York, NY 10020.

VOCABULARY

Below we'll mention a few useful Portuguese words which will appear repeatedly in the itineraries as we describe some of the sights along the way.

IN THE CITY: AVENIDA - an avenue, usually a larger street. BAIRRO - a district, section or neighborhood of a city, often used to describe the location of something. CALCADA - another name for a street, often a very small one. CENTRO - downtown: you frequently follow signs to the CENTRO when you arrive in a town or city. DOCA - a dock. LARGO - a square, usually a wide spot at an intersection. PRACA - a square, ranging from tiny to grand, the central ones often surrounded by the town's main official buildings. RUA - a street.

OUTSIDE THE CITY: ADEGA - a winery. AUTO-ESTRADA - a freeway (neither free nor very common in Portugal). ESTRADA - a highway. PRAIA - a beach. QUINTA - a country estate, usually private. RIO - a river; the name will follow as in RIO TEJO, River Tagus.

SIGHTS: ARTESANATO - a store which sells handicrafts; you'll find at least one in towns of any size. AZULEJOS - ceramic tiles, a ubiquitous decorative element in Portugal. The craft of making the tiles was extremely advanced during the Moorish occupation of the Peninsula and in Portugal endured long afterward. CABO - a cape: there are many of these along the Atlantic coast which provide wonderful views over the ocean. CASTELO - a castle, often with extensive fortifications sheltering a town and a church within. MERCADO - a market which may sell everything from fish to furniture, and is often held in the main square. MIRADOURO - a viewpoint with special views. MUSEU - a museum. PACO - a palace which was never a royal palace. PALACIO - a (former) royal palace. PELOURINHO - literally a pillory where transgressors were hanged or burned at the stake during the Inquisition. In fact, many of the pillories (there's one in almost every important town) were merely erected as a symbol of the town's authority and much care went into their design and carving. PONTE - a bridge. SOLAR - a manor house. TORRE - a tower. TORRE DE MENAGEM - a castle keep, the strongest, innermost and usually tallest tower. VISTA - a view.

RELIGIOUS PLACES: CAPELA - a chapel. CONVENTO - a convent. IGREJA MATRIZ - a parish church. MOSTEIRO - a monastery. SE - a cathedral.

SOME NAMES AND TITLES: DOM - a title of honor reserved in Portugal (unlike in Spain) for royalty and high ecclesiastical officials. DONA (the feminine) also exists but was never much used. NOSSA SENHORA (N.S.) - Our Lady (the Virgin Mary), used in the names of most churches, as in NOSSA SENHORA DA ASSUNCAO, Our Lady of the Assumption. RAINHA - a queen. REI (a king) also exists but was seldom used, DOM being preferred. SAO (S.), SANTO (STO.) - male saints. SANTA (STA.) - a female saint.

AND DON'T FORGET: DESCULPE - Excuse me. OBRIGADO (male speaker) and OBRIGADA (female) - Thank you. POR FAVOR - Please. BOM DIA - Good morning. BOA TARDE - Good afternoon. BOA NOITE - Good evening. ADEUS - Goodbye.

Lisbon Highlights

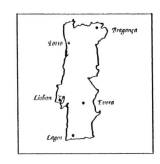

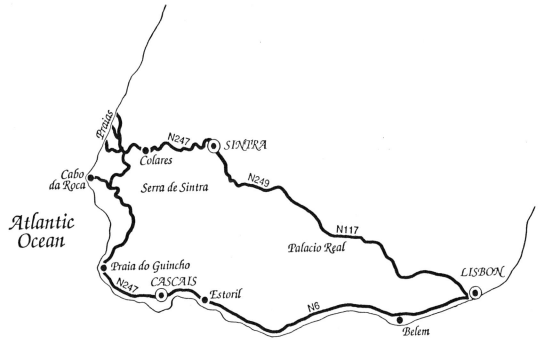

Lisbon Highlights

Any trip to Portugal should include some time in the capital and largest city, LISBON. Sitting as it does on seven low hills near the mouth of the River Tagus (Tejo), it qualifies as one of the world's most beautifully situated cities. Just above Lisbon the Tagus spreads out into a seven-kilometer-wide estuary which carries it the final 16 kilometers of its 1,000-kilometer course to the Atlantic. The sunset glow on the estuary has given it the name of "Mar de Palha," or Sea of Straw. This is the centerpiece of Lisbon's charm and its most attractive feature. It also, not incidentally, provides an excellent sheltered harbor, which has been the city's most significant economic attribute and the reason for its long-term importance.

Lisbon Highlights

Lisbon was probably first settled by the Phoenicians around 1200 B.C. and, after falling to the Greeks and Carthaginians in succession, was taken by the Romans in 205 B.C. From 714 to 1147 it was in Moorish hands and became the seat of the Portuguese monarchs around 1260. It has been the capital ever since.

The city really reached its maturity in the 16th century when so many exploratory sea voyages were launched from here. The flourishing trade with the Orient which resulted from the discovery of the route around Africa made Lisbon the European center of such commerce and brought a high level of prosperity to the city.

In 1755 an exceptionally violent earthquake hit the city and much of it was reduced to rubble, especially the lower town. The subsequent tidal wave bore away thousands of people and uncontrollable fires completed the city-wide destruction. The quake was a major event in Europe and dampened the rational optimism which prevailed at the time. The Foreign Minister serving under the inexperienced King Jose I is known as the Marques de Pombal, and the tragedy served as his springboard to nearly dictatorial power. He immediately began the reconstruction of the city following the fashionable design of the time: large streets laid out in a square pattern. The reconstruction was mostly limited to the flatter, lower town: the hillsides still retain the winding lanes of the original city.

Driving in Lisbon, as in any large European city, can be trying to say the least. We strongly suggest using taxis, plentiful and inexpensive, where walking is not possible. If your plans include car rental, our advice is to take delivery after seeing Lisbon. A good way to begin your visit to the capital is to take one of the numerous city tours, which will acquaint you with Lisbon's layout and give you an idea of which sights you wish to return to at your own leisure.

The center of business activity is the district known as the Baixa, or lower town. This is the area between the Praca do Comercio on the river bank, through Dom

Pedro IV Square (called the Rossio) and along the expansive Avenida da Liberdade to the Praca do Marques de Pombal. The Praca do Comercio is a gigantic nine-acre square (now a parking lot, unfortunately) surrounded by mostly government buildings, with an equestrian statue of King Jose I in the middle. You may hear or see the name "Terreiro do Paco" in reference to it: that means Palace Square and refers to a palace destroyed by the earthquake. Just off the southeast corner of the square is the ferry dock where you can take a boat to the city of BARREIRO on the left bank of the Tagus. From another dock just east of there you can take a tranquil 2-hour cruise on the river and glean a unique perspective of the city. It leaves daily at 2:45 (but check the time, since change is not unknown).

The area north of the square (reached through a baroque triumphal arch) consists of Lisbon's major shopping streets, which feed into the Praca like spokes. Pombal's intent was to organize the district by product category, hence names such as Rua do Ouro for the goldsmiths and Rua da Prata for the silversmiths. The distinction is no longer maintained, however, and all kinds of vendors are found on all the streets.

At the north end of this bustling area is the Rossio, or Dom Pedro IV Square, where its namesake stands atop a 75-foot column between baroque fountains. At the end of the square is the national theater with a statue of Gil Vicente, considered to be the father of Portuguese theater. He occupies a literary position in Portuguese similar to that of Shakespeare in English, though more than a century earlier.

Beyond the theater is the Restauradores Square honoring the uprising in 1640 which put an end to the Spanish occupation of Portugal. This lively square forms one end of the magnificent Liberty Avenue parkway (the Avenida da Liberdade), lined with trees, tall, modern office buildings and hotels. At the other end of the avenue is a monument to Pombal and, behind it, the elegant Edward VII Park created in honor of the 1902 visit of that English king. There are formal gardens and splendid views from the upper end of the park. Also on the west side is the Estufa Fria, a greenhouse with luxuriant tropical vegetation amid pools and waterfalls.

A couple of blocks north of the park you will find the Gulbenkian Foundation, established by the Armenian oilman who lived much of his life in Portugal and bequeathed his fortune to establish the foundation. The organization supports cultural activities and the building houses two museums. The Calouste Gulbenkian Museum contains the superior and eclectic personal collection of the benefactor: Ancient Egypt, Greece and Rome are represented along with a large collection of oriental art. The other museum has been open only a couple of years and dedicates its three floors solely to contemporary artists - both Portuguese and foreign.

To the west of the Baixa is the section known as the Bairro Alto, or upper town. An easy way to get there is to take the funicular from the Avenida da Liberdade (you'll see the station at the north end of the Praca dos Restauradores). It runs up the street called Calcada da Gloria, at the top of which is the belvedere of Sao Pedro de Alcantara overlooking striking panoramas of the city to the north. Down the Rua da Misericordia to the south is the 16th-century Sao Roque church which has a handsome, intimate interior. Attached to the church is a worthwhile museum of religious art. A little farther in the same direction lies the Square of Luis de Camoes (he wrote "The Lusiads," Portugal's greatest epic poem). To the left runs the Rua Garrett, also known as the Chiado - an elegant, animated commercial street lined with shops and cafes. If you follow it to its end and turn left on Rua do Carmo, in addition to more boutiques, you'll come across ruins of a Carmelite church (to the left). Built in the 14th century, it mostly collapsed in the earthquake. To the right is an Eiffel-designed elevator which will take you back down to the Rua do Ouro in the Baixa.

The area to the east of the Baixa is the medieval city crowned by the Sao Jorge Castle. The section nearest the river is known as the Alfama and is characterized by ancient stepped streets winding through picturesque old houses with wrought-iron balconies and washing hanging to dry from flower-bedecked windows.   At the edge near the Praca do Comercio is the Lisbon Cathedral (Se), a late 12th-century edifice largely restored after the earthquake.   It contains several small chapels and an impressive Treasury (Tesouro).   A bit farther up on the Rua Limoeiro is the Santa Luzia belvedere with superb views over the rooftops of the ancient Alfama and the rest of the city beyond.

At the apex of the hill is the castle of Sao Jorge, built on the site of the earliest town settlement.   Originally converted from a Moorish castle, it has been remodelled many times over the centuries.   There are terrific vistas from the terrace and castle battlements over the city's hills and the Tagus.   The fancy restaurant within the old castle is operated by the pousada chain, and is popular enough to merit a reservation.

A few hundred yards east of the castle is Sao Vicente de Fora church which has some beautiful azulejos in the adjoining cloisters.   In the former refectory of the attached monastery is the Royal Pantheon of the House of Braganca, containing the family tombs from that famous royal line since the 17th century. Right across the street from the church is an attractive, intimate restaurant, O Vicentinho, serving delicious regional dishes.   If you are here on Tuesday or Saturday, seek out the colorful flea markets in progress in nearby Campo de Santa Clara and Campo Santana.

Along the river to the west of the Praco do Comercio on the Rua das Janelas Verdes is the excellent Museu de Arte Antiga (Ancient Art).   Besides a first-rate collection of Portuguese art, there are good works by Spanish, Flemish and German artists.   The gold- and silversmith work is also superior, as is the exhibit of antique furniture.   This museum is definitely worth a visit.

Several kilometers to the west of the city is the Belem district, reached by car, cab or train.   You will pass under the approach to Europe's longest suspension bridge, the 25 de Abril (commemorating the Revolution of 1974), its kilometer-long span towering 200 feet above the Tagus and strongly reminiscent of the Golden Gate in San Francisco. Across the steet to the north of the Praca do Albuquerque is the rose-colored Belem Palace, where the President of Portugal resides. In the former riding school of the palace is the popular Coach Museum with unusual exhibits of royal carriages from the 16th to the 19th centuries.

Just beyond the palace is the famous Hieronymite Monastery, considered a masterpiece of Manueline architecture with its impressive St. Mary's church and an awe-inspiring cloister with elegant, sculpted arcades. King Manuel I commissioned this marvel as a gesture of gratitude for Vasco da Gama's discovery of the route to India, which resulted in the glorious era of Portuguese wealth and prominence. In the former dormitory flanking the church is the National Archaeology Museum with an impressive collection of prehistoric Iberian material. Farther west is the Naval Museum, which will appeal to those who enjoy historical displays of model ships.

Belem Tower

Across the grassy Imperial Square in front of the monastery are two reminders of the past: the five-story Belem Tower and the Monument to the Discoveries. The former was constructed as a fortress in the early 16th century in the middle of the Tagus, which obviously has changed course a bit, since the tower now sits on the right bank.   The monument was erected in 1960, on the 500th anniversary of the death of Prince Henry the Navigator, who opened the doors to the 16th-century period of discovery.   Between the two is a museum of folk art and crafts from around Portugal.

As for dining out in Lisbon, the following restaurants are popular, quite expensive and easy to recommend: the AVIZ on Rua Serpa Pinto, 12B; the GAMBRINUS on Rua das Portas da Santa Antao, 23; the O PAGEM on Largo da Trinidade, 20; the TAGIDE on Largo da Academia Nacional de Belas Artes, 18; and, our special favorite, the CASA DA COMIDA on Travessa das Amoreiras, 1.

EXCURSIONS FROM LISBON: There are a number of ways to see the "Portuguese Riviera," which is the name given to the area to the west of the city, between Lisbon and the Atlantic.   Numerous guided tours are available by bus, although their one-day duration can't really do justice to this beautiful area.   Another way, of course, is by car from Lisbon.   Finally, there is excellent train service from Lisbon to CASCAIS-ESTORIL and from Lisbon to SINTRA.   In fact, if you are not particularly enamored of the hustle and bustle of city visits, you might seriously consider choosing one of the lovely hotels in Cascais or Sintra (see the hotel listings) and make Lisbon the excursion from there - the trains make the 35-minute trip to the capital every half-hour between 5:30am and 10:00pm and every hour 10:00pm to 2:00am.   The Sintra route takes you right to the Rossio in the center of town, and the Cascais train arrives at the Estacao do Cais Sodre, a few blocks west of the Praca do Comercio.   A return to the relative calm and amenities particular to a seaside hotel is not a bad way to end a day of city sightseeing.   Be sure to confirm the train schedules at the hotel desk, since they may change.

If you opt to stay in Lisbon, below is a description of the route from there by car:

ESTORIL-CASCAIS: Leave Lisbon heading west on the Avenida 24 de Julho along the river. After passing the 25 de Abril Bridge, the road name changes to the Avenida da India. Beyond the Belem Tower you are on the corniche road N6. Another 20 kilometers along first the Tagus, then the Atlantic, and past several small resorts brings you to ESTORIL.

The old-world resort of Estoril has been a favorite stomping ground of the European jet set for a century. The once-magnificent beaches have deteriorated somewhat through use, but you'll still be impressed by the lovely private villas and the large central park filled with exotic plants. This coastal area enjoys an especially mild climate all year round. All sorts of activities, outdoor and indoor, from golf to gambling, abound in this somewhat exclusive resort town.

Although separate technically, Estoril now forms a contiguous developed unit with CASCAIS, former summer home of the Portuguese royal family (19th century), and now that of the President. Originally a tiny fishing village, today it is a pleasant and colorful resort town resplendent with shops, restaurants and flowery parks. The calm bay provides fine views and good sailing.

Just out of town on the coast road (N247-8) is a giant sea-formed abyss called BOCA DO INFERNO (Hell's Jaws). Breakers smash into the rocky caverns creating intriguing patterns among the oddly shaped rocks of the promontory. As you continue along this road you'll be treated to spectacular ocean views. You come upon a good viewpoint at CABO RASO, then skirt the long PRAIA DO GUINCHO with its forested borders (warning: there is said to be a strong undertow here). Another six kilometers brings you to a junction for MALVEIRA, where you turn left and enter the lower edge of the beautiful, wooded SERRA DA SINTRA. Watch for a left turn onto N247-4 which leads out to CABO DA ROCA, the westernmost point of the European continent - an isolated, elevated promontory from which to survey the vastness of the Atlantic.

Return to N247 and turn left. You are still skirting the western edge of the Serra and will shortly come upon the little town of COLARES, justly famous for its superior wines. The cooperative there is open to the public and makes a tasty stop. Following N375 southwest will take you through the lush, green hills of the Sintra region. After a few kilometers on the tranquil country road, a large stone arch at the entrance to the Palacio de Seteais (seven sighs) will catch your eye. The Palace is now a luxury hotel (see the hotel listings), and has a good restaurant, in case you happen to be driving by at mealtime. Soon afterward you reach SINTRA (often spelled CINTRA in English).

Just as you enter town, you'll see a sign to the right, leading up a narrow, zig-zagging lane to the Castelo dos Mouros and the Palacio da Pena. The castle dates from the 7th century and its remains lurk down dark paths beneath dense vegetation, its ramparts providing enchanting views of the Serra. A kilometer up the road is the fantastic 19th-century palace, a colorful, flight-of-fancy construction with elements of every architectural period imaginable. There are guided tours of the interior, featuring art objects and furnishings supposedly left exactly as they were when the monarchy was overthrown in 1910. The terraces, guard paths and ornate onion dome afford marvelous views to Lisbon and the Tagus to the east and the Atlantic to the west.

In Sintra is another National Palace near the middle of town on the Praca da Republica. This one was originally built in the 14th century as a royal residence and subsequently much remodelled. Guided tours will take you through its wonderfully furnished rooms and halls.

The town itself offers peaceful, pleasant walks, shopping and a variety of good restaurants. In addition, it's surprisingly cool in the summertime. Lord Byron resided here for a while in the early 19th century and it is easy to see why he chose this beautiful location.

Leave Sintra on N249 and, after about 15 kilometers, watch for the turnoff to QUELUZ, where you'll discover the rococo Palacio Nacional de Queluz, a beautiful, former summer palace of the Braganca royal house. It is still used for formal state occasions. Its 18th-century style includes Versailles-like formal gardens and a particularly harmonious blend of decorative elements inside.

Returning to the main road, N117, it's only eight kilometers to Lisbon, which you enter through the Monsanto Forest Park on the western edge of the city.

Sintra
Palacio da Pema

The Alluring Algarve

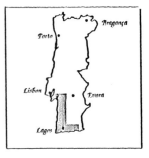

Lisbon
Rio Tejo
Palmela
Setúbal
Marateca
E4
N10
N10
N5
Rio Sado
AZEITÃO
Alcácer do Sal
N120
Atlantic
Ocean
Grândola
▲ Miróbriga
SANTIAGO DE CACEM
Sines
N120-1
Porto Covo
Tanganheira
Cercal
Vila Nova
de Milfontes
N120
Odemira
Odeceixe
MONCHIQUE
Fóia
Porto de Lagos
Portimão
N266
Alfambras
São Bras de Alportel
N268
N125
Guia
N270
Loulé
Milreu
Tavira
Vila do Bispo
N125
Figueira
Lagos
Praia
da Rocha
Praia
de Gale
Albufeira
SANTA
BARBARA
DE NEXE
Faro
Olhão
Cabo S. Vicente
SAGRES

49

The Alluring Algarve

This itinerary takes you to one of Portugal's most popular tourist areas: the southern strip called the Algarve. The name comes from the Arabic word for west, so-called because it was the most westerly European stronghold of the brilliant Islamic civilization that occupied most of the Peninsula during the Middle Ages. Due to its somewhat isolated geographical situation - separated from the rest of the country by a chain of mountains - it was both the first area taken by the Moors and the last to be regained by the Christians, thus spending the longest time under Arab domination. As might be expected, it retains the greatest cultural influence of that civilization.

Cape St. Vincent

That same geographical circumstance provides it with protection from the colder northern weather, so the 100-mile strip between the wild, craggy cliffs of Cape St. Vincent on the west and the bucolic deltas of the Spanish border on the east enjoys a warm climate all year round. These favorable climatic conditions have given rise to an internationally popular string of resort areas along the Atlantic beaches, which the Portuguese call the Costa do Sol (sun coast). While less blighted with high-rise condominiums than Spain's Costa del Sol, the Algarve offers everything from quaint fishing villages to swanky resorts and casinos, along with ample opportunities for all kinds of outdoor activities from sports to sunbathing.

Although restaurants offering a variety of international cuisines can be found in the larger towns, due to its strong fishing tradition, the Algarve's forte is its cornucopia of fresh seafood dishes. The ubiquitous "caldeirada de peixe" (bouillabaisse) comes in as many forms as there are chefs. Various mixtures of fish and shellfish are prepared "a cataplana" (a lidded, round-bottomed skillet) over an open flame. Versions of this concoction also include cured ham and/or pork along with the typical clams and other fish.

Although the Algarve is your ultimate destination, driving there is a pleasure. You'll explore picturesque byways and visit ancient castles crowning hilltops over terraced towns. Most of the route stays within sight of the Atlantic shore with panoramic views stretching forever from rugged promontories.

You will also visit one of Portugal's most revered historical sites: Sagres, where Henry the Navigator prepared Portuguese sailors for the astounding voyages of discovery to the Orient. In addition to the coast, this itinerary takes you into the crystal clear air and lush vegetation of the Serra de Monchique to a charming mountain town with equally charming accommodations.

When you have finished sampling the delights of Lisbon, you can continue your Portuguese holiday by venturing south to investigate the temptations of the cosmopolitan Algarve.

DESTINATION I   AZEITAO   Quinta das Torres

Leave Lisbon on the freeway heading south toward SETUBAL, crossing the impressive 25th of April suspension bridge - reminiscent of San Francisco's Golden Gate - which soars 200 feet above the River Tagus.   The views from the bridge looking back toward Lisbon are fabulous, but since there is no place to stop, the driver won't have much chance to see them.   However, an equally impressive view is yours for the picture-taking from the Cristo-Rei statue in ALMADA (watch for the exit just after leaving the bridge).   The statue was built by the bishops of Portugal in 1959 in thanks for Portugal's non-involvement in World War II and stands nearly 400 feet above the river.   The statue itself is not particularly interesting but the city vista is unforgettable.

Return to the freeway and continue south to the N10 exit toward Setubal, where a short 14-kilometer drive brings you to AZEITAO.   Just beyond an intersection with the road to SESIMBRA watch for the gate on your right with a small sign announcing your hotel for tonight, the QUINTA DAS TORRES, a wonderful old farmhouse/inn converted from a 16th-century noble palace and set in luxuriant gardens.

Nearby NOGUEIRA DE AZEITAO is the home of Portugal's internationally famous Lancers wine, produced under the Jose Maria da Fonseca label. The winery (adega) also produces an excellent dry white (Branco Seco B.S.E.) and a fine, full red (Dao Terras Altas). On weekdays from 9:00 to 11:30 and 2:00 to 5:00, the adega welcomes visitors for tours and wine tasting - an experience that shouldn't be missed. The visit includes a small museum housing an interesting collection of wine glasses and 17th- and 18th-century azulejos (ceramic tiles).

Quinta das Torres
Azeitao

If you happen to be in town on the first Sunday of the month, be sure to seek out the colorful local market in Azeitao.

The ocean and mountain scenery of this region is spectacular and, time permitting, we suggest you allow a day to poke around and enjoy it. (For a recommended route, see the next itinerary.)

Today's journey takes you to Portugal's third-largest seaport, after Lisbon and Porto, and to the heart of the cork-producing region - cork being one of the country's biggest exports.

Take N10 east from Azeitao to the bustling port of SETUBAL.   As you approach you can't miss the 16th-century Castle of Sao Filipe towering above town; it now houses a pousada and affords panoramic views of the city and bay from its ramparts.   The castle was commissioned by Phillip II of Spain during the period when the two nations were ruled by the same monarch.   The dining room here offers particularly good regional specialties, especially if you like seafood, and would make a fine stop for lunch.   Be sure to see (on your left as you ascend the broad stairs to the pousada entrance) the castle's tiny chapel, every interior inch of which is covered with deep blue-and-white azulejos.

The Setubal area has been an important settlement since Roman times.   Its predecessor, the Roman town of Cetobriga, is thought to have been across the estuary.   In addition to its port facilities and the nearby shipyards at SETENAVE, it is a significant salt-manufacturing center.

The most interesting part of the city is the old town center around Bocage Square.   (Bocage, one of Portugal's most famous poets, was born in Setubal in the 18th century.)   You'll enjoy the picturesque winding streets and alleyways, some of which have been converted to pedestrian-only use.   A couple of blocks northeast of the square is the Municipal Museum, housed in a 17th-century convent.   The 15th-century Igreja de Jesus adjoining it is thought to be the earliest example of that highly Portuguese-style, late-Gothic architecture called Manueline, named for King Manuel I.

Across the estuary from Setubal is the burgeoning resort area of TROIA, which may be reached by ferry or hovercraft, either with or without your car (though there is little reason to take a car). Check with the tourist office on Bocage Square for current schedules and departure points. The peninsula boasts what is reputedly the longest fine, white-sand beach in the country - nearly 20 miles. If you take the trip, don't miss visiting the ruins of Cetobriga.

When you are ready to leave, take N10 east to MARATECA, where you join N5 and head south to ALCACER DO SAL. The road winds through forests of pine and cork oaks - the latter often with bare, gnarled trunks, the result of being stripped of their bark. You're likely to see loads of brown cork stacked high on both trucks and horse-drawn carts as you drive through this region. Portugal is the world's largest producer of this seemingly minor but almost indispensable commodity.

The quaint agricultural town of Alcacer do Sal is dominated by the ruins of a Moorish castle occupying a broad hill overlooking the Sado River. Houses on cobblestone streets crowd right up to the castle walls. If time permits, you might want to stop long enough to experience the ancient flavor of the old town.

Continue south on N120 another 23 kilometers to the little country town of GRANDOLA, a hub of the cork industry. Follow the signs for SANTIAGO DO CACEM through town, after which a pretty, twisting 25-kilometer drive through the hilly, green Serra de Grandola will bring you to today's destination.

Just before you reach the town of Santiago, a sign for MIROBRIGA on the left leads you about one kilometer to the partially excavated ruins of that Roman town. Archaeological findings here indicate that the settlement was built on the site of a previous late-Neolithic center which, by the 3rd century B.C., was occupied by the Celts. There is a small municipal museum at the site displaying some of the artifacts found during excavation.

Pousada de Sao Tiago
Santiago do Cacem

Back on the main road, shortly beyond the turnoff to the ruins, is tonight's hotel: the POUSADA DE SAO TIAGO. Its name is simply an alternate spelling of Santiago, or St. James. The cozy little inn is just outside the town proper in a park-like setting, with a wonderful view of Santiago.

The town itself is built on a hillside crowned by a Moorish castle, rebuilt by the Knights Templar, whose walls now enclose a cemetery. The original Moorish castle, called Cacem (probably the name of a person), was recaptured by the Templars in the 12th century and subsequently lost to the Moors again. When the area was definitively recaptured by the Christians in the 13th century, it was donated by the King to the Order of Santiago. The ramparts afford fine views of the town and surrounding area. Next to the castle is the colorful 13th-century Igreja Matriz (parish church) with a 14th-century relief of Sao Tiago battling the Moors.

As you leave Santiago heading toward SINES, be sure to look back for an impressive view of its well-preserved castle.   The former fishing village of Sines has been transformed into a cluster of high-tech petrochemical installations which, in a curious juxtaposition, overshadow ancient farms and horse-drawn carts.   This was the birthplace of Vasco da Gama, one of Portugal's greatest heroes in the age of the great explorations.   Due to its recent industrialization, the town has little charm.

Take the exit (marked SUL ALGARVE and CERCAL) from the freeway before reaching Sines to get onto N120-1.   After a few kilometers watch for a road to the right leading six kilometers to PORTO COVO, a small fishing village with an unusual red, white and blue town square and colorful houses leading down to the edge of the sea.   From here you can see the tiny island of PESSEGUEIRA, the ruins of a fort crowning its rocky formation.   You'll notice numerous routes to the coast as you approach town, each offering a different perspective and the chance to explore the pretty coves that dot the shoreline.

As you leave Porto Covo the way you came, watch carefully for a road to the right with a sign indicating, among other places, VILA NOVA DE MILFONTES. Although the road is not on the Michelin map, it saves several kilometers in reaching that developing little resort town at the mouth of the Mira River.   The road runs mostly through cultivated farmland, keeping the sea in sight, and ends at a junction with N390 where you turn right.   If you miss the shortcut, you can return to N120, turn right, then take N390 at the little town of CERCAL to arrive at the same place.   In either case, turn right before crossing the bridge to get to the town proper.   On the water's edge is a small, ivy-covered, fortified castle built by King Joao IV in the 17th century.   The castle is now a charming guest house CASTELO DE MILFONTES and cannot be visited as a tourist site.

The town itself is prettily situated on a promontory over the river estuary.

Return to N390 and turn right across the bridge to pick up N393. After a fairly quick 23 kilometers you regain N120 just south of ODEMIRA. Another 23 kilometers, with pretty landscapes as the distant Serra de Monchique comes into view on your left, brings you to ODECEIXE. The bridge into town marks the delineation between the Lower Alentejo province and the Algarve. As you go deeper into this region, the landscape and architecture take on a distinctive Mediterranean flavor, with towns painted white against the heat, and tropical vegetation.

Pousada Do Infante
Sagres

Continuing on N120, you descend to ALJEZUR with its Moorish castle ruins, then ALFAMBRAS, where N268 runs along the edge of the Serra de Espinhaco de Cao ("dog's backbone") toward VILA DO BISPO. Another 10 kilometers bring you to your destination for tonight, SAGRES, and the dramatic POUSADA DO INFANTE (Infante = Prince), precariously situated atop a rugged cliff overlooking the Atlantic. You'll see the white hotel on a promontory to the left when you reach the crossroads at the edge of town.

Along with fishing and diving, a popular pastime in this area, as you will soon see, is to rent bicycles in the quaint village of Sagres and tour the area out to the cape. The secluded beaches in this area, punctuated with the craggy rock outcroppings so strongly associated with the Algarve, make attractive destinations, especially at sunset.

The once world-famous school of seafaring on this windswept, barren tip of the European continent was the scene of some of the most exciting advances in navigation, cartography and sailing technology during the 15th century. The progress made here in these areas under the direction of Prince Henry the Navigator (O Infante Dom Henrique o Navegador) made possible the great voyages of discovery to the Cape of Good Hope at the southern tip of Africa (Bartolomeo Dias in 1488) and, ultimately, to India (Vasco da Gama in 1498). The Portuguese thus accomplished what Columbus failed to do and opened a sea route from Europe to the spice-rich Orient. Most of the school's original buildings were destroyed by the famous English pirate, Sir Francis Drake, during his 1597 sack of Lagos.

On a promontory to the west of the pousada is the fort where Prince Henry's school is said to have been located. On the ground in the courtyard is an immense "rosa dos ventos," or compass rose, constructed of stone, supposedly used for instruction during Prince Henry's time. In addition, there is a small exhibit, and sometimes a film, on the events of the Age of Discovery (inquire about the showtime for the English-language version). There is also a youth hostel within the fort grounds.

A few kilometers farther west is the little 17th-century fort of BELICHE, now a delightful tea-room and restaurant with four bedrooms operated by the pousada chain (see the hotel listings for more details).

Just beyond is Cape St. Vincent, the most southwestern point in Europe. This rocky promontory has been the scene of numerous sea battles throughout the history of Portugal, guarding as it does the entrance to the narrow channel into the Mediterranean.   Giant fingers of rock jut out into the ocean where they are battered by crashing waves.   The view is breathtaking and, considering the wild setting, it's easy to see how earlier Europeans might have equated this desolate spot with the end of the earth.   You can climb the lighthouse installed in an old convent for an even more panoramic view of the Atlantic.   The cape's name stems from the legend that the remains of St. Vincent, Portugal's patron saint, washed ashore here before later reappearing in Lisbon.

DESTINATION IV   MONCHIQUE   Hotel Mons Cicus

When you are ready to depart the relative isolation of Sagres for the more lively Algarve, return to Vila do Bispo and turn right on N125.   The road along here runs a short distance inland from the coast, but frequent signs beckon you to investigate the hidden beaches and coves just south.   These beaches (e.g. Praia da Salema and Praia da Luz) are less populated than those nearer FARO, but they don't offer the quantity of shops and restaurants associated with the more frequented areas.   If seclusion is your style, you might want to explore the possibilities here.

About 20 kilometers from Vila do Bispo you approach the small resort town of LAGOS, once the embarkation point for Africa.   Just before town is a sign for the Praia de Dona Ana, a beach uniquely situated beneath giant red cliffs eroded into impressive shapes by ceaseless waves.

The tree-lined Avenida dos Descobrimentos (discoveries) separates Lagos from the sea.   Most of the early voyages departed from these shores, and Prince Henry called it home for a while.   As you enter town, there's a small fort on the right, and beyond to the left is the Praca da Republica, with a statue of Prince

Henry the Navigator. For strolling, the area between this square and the Praca de Gil Eanes to the east, marked with a statue of Dom Sebastiao, is the most interesting.

Dom Sebastiao, King of Portugal from 1557 to 1578, was reportedly slain at the battle of Alcacer Kebir on an ill-advised expedition against the Moslems of Africa. The young, handsome king was only 24 (a regent had ruled in his name for some time). Since no one witnessed his death, a cult called Sebastianism evolved, which proclaimed that the popular monarch did not actually die, and would someday return to rule Portugal. The belief gave rise to numerous imposters claiming to be Sebastiao and offering themselves as king. His death paved the way for the succession of Spain's Phillip II to the throne of Portugal, forcing it to be part of the hated Spanish Empire. Sebastiao's death is generally seen as the end of Portugal's period of glory, since after 80 years of Spanish domination, the country required another 60 to rebuild after the War of Liberation.

Leave Lagos heading east on N125 for the 18 kilometers to PORTIMAO, an industrious fishing port situated at the mouth of the Arade River. Just south of town is PRAIA DA ROCHA, one of the coast's original beach resorts, evidenced by the old mansions and villas along the shore.

If you are in Portimao at lunch time, look for the sign for the Dennis Inn just behind the main square, about halfway through town along the port road. Unfortunately, the bedrooms were out of service when we were there, but the restaurant is open and excellent, offering one of the most interesting and creative menus in Portugal. Even better, if you can make it here for dinner, by all means do. There is live entertainment every night amidst a lively, congenial atmosphere (during our visit it was singalong Irish folk music). The delightful owners Ann Lancaster and Pierre Larocque are Canadians who visited the Algarve once on holiday and came back for good.

Hotel Mons Cicus
Monchique

Leave Portimao heading north on N124 to PORTO DE LAGOS where you take a left on N266 into the Serra de Monchique. Eleven winding, green kilometers bring you to CALDAS DE MONCHIQUE (caldas = mineral baths), a tiny summer resort town. Six kilometers farther is MONCHIQUE, built on the mountainside surrounded by kaleidoscopic vistas over the surrounding hills and terraced fields. To reach your hotel, continue in the direction of FOIA (following the signs from the center of town). As you ascend the steep incline, you pass the hotel ABRIGO DA MONTANHA (see the listings), shortly after which will appear a sign for the HOTEL MONS CICUS to the left, just beyond and across the road from the Restaurante Rampa. The setting here is truly spectacular and you will love the beautiful hotel and its wonderful views to the sea.

Monchique is known for its local handicrafts, the most notable being wicker baskets, leather goods, copper and brass items, woolen sweaters, and heavy woven-wool spreads which would make handsome bedcovers or rugs. There is also attractive, unfinished wood furniture. You will find all these products in the many little shops around town.

Though it's difficult to depart the tranquil mountain setting, today's itinerary unveils the more cosmopolitan part of the Algarve, as well as a wonderful hotel away from the hustle and bustle of the coastal resorts.

Leave Monchique the way you came on N266 and turn left on N269 at Porto de Lagos to reach SILVES.   This dramatically situated town with its dark, 12th-century battlements high over the river was once the capital of the Moorish Al-Gharb, rivalling Granada in splendor and culture.   Now it's a small town with some handsome burghers' houses in the shadow of a Moorish castle.

Head south on N124 to the fishing village of LAGOA where you turn left on N125. At GUIA follow the signs for a right turn toward ALBUFEIRA, a bustling seaside fishing village turned resort.   It boasts a large, usually busy beach, which is reached by a tunnel from the main square in town.   The predominantly white buildings are colorfully decorated with bright awnings.   Shops and restaurants abound here as do street vendors with multi-hued umbrellas covering their wares. It's an inviting place to stroll around the steep streets and inspect the shops and attractive cafes.   You might even want to try the beach if you came prepared; if not, you will certainly enjoy a break at one of the beachfront cafes.

Return to the N125 and turn right toward FARO.   Along the highway are numerous local-handicraft shops, featuring mainly ceramic, tin and brass wares. If you want an unusual typical item to take home, you might buy a "cataplana," a brass frying pan with an attached lid.   Otherwise, as the ocean is not visible from the highway, this drive to the Algarve's major city is unremarkable.   Faro gets its name from its Moorish founder, Ben Haroun, but its buildings date mostly from the 18th century.   In 1596 the British, on an expedition against Spain, sacked and burned the city to the ground.   After it was rebuilt, the 1755 earthquake levelled it again, so the architecture is relatively recent. It is now an industrial town with few attractions beyond the port area with its tree-lined avenues. At the north end of the harbor is a Maritime Museum with models of boats and ships. The area to the east of the harbor is the traditional downtown area with shops and pedestrian streets. The Faro beach - actually an offshore strip of sand - is about nine kilometers by car, or can be reached by ferry (from June to September) from the Porta Nova pier in the harbor.

From Faro, take N2 north toward Sao Bras De Alportel and, after about 10 kilometers, watch for signs for the Roman ruins of MILREU, at a crossroad near the town of ESTOI. The small site is thought to be the Roman predecessor of Faro and merits a brief visit.

To reach your hotel for tonight, follow the same road west across N2 toward SANTA BARBARA DE NEXE. As you reach the small hill town, watch for signs to the HOTEL LA RESERVE, just beyond to the west. Here you can relax in luxury while relishing some of the finest cuisine in the country, as well as splendid vistas over the hills to the sea from your private terrace.

Hotel La Reserve
Santa Barbara de Nexe

If and when you can tear yourself away from the restaurant and lovely pool, there are some noteworthy attractions within driving distance to consider. Between Faro and Albufeira are numerous beaches worth exploring. In the VILAMOURA-QUARTEIRA area is a long stretch of sand sheltered by red cliffs and home to all kinds of nautical sports, several golf courses, a casino, nightclubs, elegant shops and a variety of restaurants.

About 10 kilometers northwest lies the picturesque mountain village of LOULE, known for its local handicrafts and its collection of intricately carved chimneys, so characteristic of the Algarve.

Only eight kilometers north on N2 is SAO BRAS DE ALPORTEL, where you can have lunch in one of Portugal's earliest pousadas (see the hotel listings) and gaze over the town rooftops to Faro and the sea beyond. The town has given its name to a dish that is popular in all of Portugal: Bacalhau a Bras, a mixture of dried salt cod, eggs, onion and potatoes. The result is a tasty (and hearty) combination.

On N125 east of Faro are OLHAO and TAVIRA, two relatively unspoiled fishing villages. The former has a pretty waterfront park and promenade. The latter is more colorful and boasts a Roman bridge over the Asseca River. It's a great place for strolling around to soak up the authentic feel of a traditional Algarvian town.

Arrabida
Convento di Arrabida

66

Exploring the Alentejo

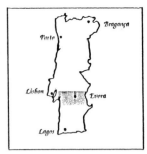

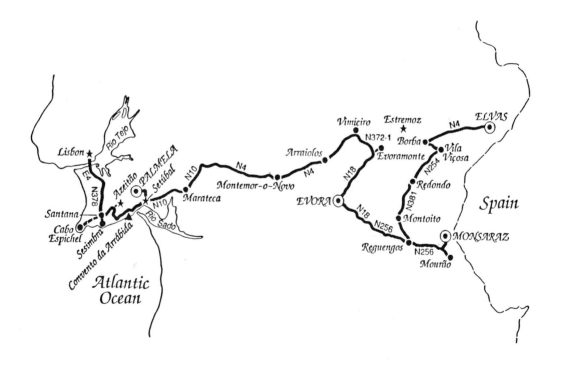

Exploring the Alentejo

After a drive along the Costa de Lisboa and some spectacular views of the Atlantic, this itinerary takes you into the heart of the Upper Alentejo region, which preserves some of the country's prettiest and most interesting historical towns. The area is also known as the "granary of Portugal," and is primarily devoted to agriculture. Its population is relatively sparse, with isolated white farm buildings occupying the low hills in the middle of seemingly endless cultivated fields.

Most of the itinerary follows the major route from Lisbon to Spain - through Badajoz - so the main roads are pretty good. For the same reason, you'll be seeing some of the most heavily fortified villages and castles in the country. Throughout much of the Peninsula's early history the two countries were constantly threatening to encroach on each other's turf. Defense spending was definitely a high priority for many early Portuguese monarchs.

Palmela Castle

Exploring the Alentejo

You will have the opportunity to stay in three of Portugal's most impressive pousadas, as well as a tiny inn located in a fortified hilltop town. The hotels are sightseeing attractions in their own right, and situated in picturesque towns which impart the flavor of medieval Portugal.

ORIGINATING CITY   LISBON

Lisbon is an attractive city and pleasant to visit, but since it was mostly leveled by an earthquake in 1755, it is characterized by fairly recent architecture and design.   Other parts of Portugal were less affected by the earthquake and thus retain more historical ambiance.   This itinerary will impart a sense of history difficult to imagine in the capital city.

DESTINATION I   PALMELA   Pda. Castelo de Palmela

Leave Lisbon on the freeway heading south across the 25th of April tollbridge and take the second exit in the direction of SESIMBRA.   Follow N378 to the little town of SANTANA, in the Arrabida Nature Park, then bear right on N379, through green fields dotted with white houses and windmills, to CABO ESPICHEL.   Past the pilgrimage chapel dedicated to Our Lady of the Cape, you walk out on a windswept, rocky promontory with magnificent views of the clear, deep-blue ocean and the rugged, craggy coast.

Head back toward Santana and take a right before town to drive by the well-restored Castle of Sesimbra.   Occupying a defensive position held by numerous masters, it is a massive square structure with turrets and towers recalling earlier battles.   There are expansive views from its ramparts of town, the sea and the surrounding countryside.   There is also a restored 18th-century church within the castle.

SESIMBRA is a colorful little fishing village with a pretty harbor nestled beneath rugged cliffs, which combine to make it an appealing spot for a little wandering. .

Return to Santana and turn right on N379, then right again after 10 kilometers on N379-1, passing through the lovely pine forests of the Serra da Arrabida. As you approach the coast you have a choice of roads.   (If you have time, the scenery merits the drive on both.)   The one to the right runs close to the coast and passes the quaint fishing-village-cum-resort of PORTINHO DA ARRABIDA and the pretty beach at FIGUEIRINHA.

The left fork winds through the mountains, affording some absolutely breathtaking views of SETUBAL, the coastline and the endless stretch of white sand across the water on the TROIA peninsula.   On the other side is a deep green valley cutting through the Serra.   This route also runs close by the dramatic 16th-century Convent of Arrabida, a walled group of buildings, like a tiny ghost town, cupped in the hillside overlooking the sea.   The convent can be seen from the lower road, but at some distance.   You could drive one way on one road, come back on the other to N379 and remain on it to PALMELA.   If time is short take either to Setubal, then head north on N252 to tonight's destination.

Whichever route you choose, the POUSADA CASTELO DE PALMELA - one of Portugal's finest - awaits you at the end of the road.   Perched atop a hill above town, the inn occupies a 15th-century convent constructed within the confines of the castle.   The stronghold was used by the Romans and the Moors and was destroyed and rebuilt numerous times throughout its history.

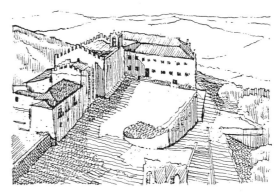

Pousada Castelo de Palmela
Palmela

Encircled by vineyards, Palmela is a picturesque white town crossed by narrow streets winding to quaint little squares. Both the Church of Sao Pedro and the Church of the Misericordia are worth a visit for their beautiful azulejo interior decoration. But, not surprisingly, the major sight is your hotel and the castle facing it. Don't miss the views from the ramparts, especially from the 14th-century keep (next to the ruins of the Church of Santa Maria, victim of the 1755 quake). The outer walls date from the 17th century, the inner ones from the 12th. The 15th-century Church of Santiago, next to the pousada, is another fine example of azulejo adornment, and its upper choir is thought to be the first built in Portugal. Walking the castle grounds is like a return to the legendary time of chivalry.

DESTINATION II   EVORA   Pda. dos Loios

Moving inland, leave Palmela on N252 south to join N10 and turn left. After 20 kilometers bear left at the junction with N5 to MARATECA. Another 14 kilometers brings up a right turn onto N4, the highway to Badajoz in Spain. This is the plains region of the country, vast expanses of undulating, cultivated land stretching in all directions. Next you will come to the Moorish-appearing white town of MONTEMOR-O-NOVO, birthplace of Sao Joao de Deus, founder of the Brothers Hospitallers, whose statue is in the church square. The medieval fortified castle above town, occupying the former site of a Roman fortress, provides good views of the olive-tree-dotted countryside.

Continue on N4, bearing left just beyond Montemor, to ARRAIOLOS, a picturesque town climbing to a 14th-century castle overlooking the Alentejo Plain for miles in all directions. A beautiful blue-and-white church shares the hilltop. Not for the last time, you'll notice that the otherwise-whitewashed houses are colorfully painted halfway up. The town is noted for its woven woolen carpets (tapetes), the continuance of a craft practiced here since the 16th century. The designs have an almost oriental quality and are done in a variety of vivid colors. Another famous local product is sausage. Just north of town is the 16th-century Convento (now Quinta) dos Loios, with a graceful Manueline church and an azulejo doorway.

Continue on N4, bypassing VIMIEIRO, and turn right on N372-1 toward EVORA. After 15 kilometers bear left toward EVORAMONTE, the site of the treaty-signing ending the war between Pedro IV and his brother Miguel. The ancient hilltop town is crowned by a 14th-century castle and has fabulous views of surrounding villages and of Estremoz to the northeast. Wind your way back down the hill and complete the 28-kilometer journey to the monumental, walled city of Evora - Portugal's pride. Tonight's hotel, the POUSADA DOS LOIOS, is in a former monastery, elegantly restored to retain the serenity required by its previous occupants.

Whitewashed, stone-framed Evora is called the "museum city" due to its quantity of historically interesting architecture. It is thought the Romans had a settlement here in the 1st century A.D. which was greatly expanded by the

Pousada dos Loios
Evora

Moors from the 8th to the 12th centuries, when Gerald the Fearless captured it for the Christians. During the next three centuries Evora was the preferred residence of the monarchs of Portugal. A Jesuit university was founded here in the mid-16th century, at the height of Evora's glory as the intellectual center of the country. When Phillip II succeeded to the Portuguese throne in 1580, he quickly annexed Evora to Spain and a long period of decline followed, although the first episode in the war of liberation against Spain occurred here in the 1630s. Today the town is a lively market center for the produce from the Alentejo Plains which surround it, and a justifiably famous tourist attraction.

Many of the major sights are around the pousada. Portugal's best-preserved Roman structure, a temple, is found right outside the door. Across the square is the art museum with one of the country's top collections, and the impressive 13th-century cathedral (called a "Se" in Portuguese), one of whose 16th-century towers has an intriguing tiled spire. Both merit a visit. To the right of the pousada entrance is the Church of St. John the Evangelist, privately owned by the Cadaval family, but sometimes open to the public (ask at the pousada desk).

This has some pretty azulejos. Past the church is the Cadaval Palace, constructed on a large section of Roman wall.

Above all, take time to stroll the ancient streets and see the marvelous medieval and Renaissance buildings. At various points you can also get views of the city walls which are of Roman, Visigothic and medieval origin.

Another must is a visit to the long main square (Praca do Giraldo), the bustling center of the town's activity, with medieval arches and a marble, Renaissance fountain - the last sight seen by the many Inquisition victims who went to the stake here. This is the main shopping district, where you might want to examine the woolen goods for which the area is so well-known.

A favorite local restaurant is O FIALHO on Travessa das Mascarenhas, in the northwestern part of town. It serves delicious regional specialties.

DESTINATIÓN III   MONSARAZ   Estalagem de Monsaraz

Today's drive is short and takes you almost to the Spanish border to an enchanting medieval village. Take N18 southeast from Evora and bear left after 16 kilometers on N256. Another 20 kilometers of fairly flat highway through rich plains studded with white farms and dusty-green olive groves, brings you to the little agricultural town of REGUENGOS DE MONSARAZ. Notice the unusual church in the town's main square. Eighteen kilometers farther on is MOURAO. The road crosses the Guadiana River, which in some stretches (though not here) marks the border between Spain and Portugal. Watch for the vantage point along the way where you can see both the hilltop town of Mourao and its sister to the north, MONSARAZ, your destination for tonight. It's obvious that defense against Spanish invasion was uppermost in the mind of King

Exploring the Alentejo

Dom Dinis when he ordered these two fortified towns constructed in the 14th century. The well-preserved castle walls in Mourao have a pretty, white parish church built into them, and afford an impressive view across the valley to Monsaraz. It's worth a short stop to explore the quaint streets of this former fortress.

Backtrack on N256 and recross the Guadiana. The roadside scenery in this major wool-producing region is pastoral and picturesque. You are likely to see flocks of sheep under the watchful eye of shepherds, traditionally clad in brown sheepskin coats whose long tails ward off damp and cold during the hours spent sitting on the ground.

Watch for a roadsign indicating a right turn to Monsaraz, which lies about seven kilometers to the north. This tiny fortified village is steeped in authentic medieval atmosphere and the simple whitewashed and blue-trimmed inn, the ESTALAGEM DE MONSARAZ, does nothing to dispel the mood.

Estalagem de Monsaraz
Monsaraz

Like Evora, Monsaraz was reclaimed from the Moors by Gerald the Fearless in the 12th century and formed an important part of the defensive scheme of subsequent Portuguese monarchs. The narrow town streets are made for wandering, and the Rua Direita, lined with ancient white houses sporting coats of arms, will transport you back in time. From the town's 13th-century castle ramparts, it's apparent why this spot was chosen for defense. The spectacular views stretch forever across the Alentejo Plain into Spain.

DESTINATION IV   ELVAS   Pda. de Santa Luzia

When you are ready to move on, return to N256 and Reguengos. Head north on N381 through MONTOITO to REDONDO, an old hilltop town which still has some of its fortifications but whose castle is in ruins. Continue another 19 kilometers on N254 to VILA VICOSA.

Once the home of the Dukes of Braganca and several Portuguese kings of the same family, Vila Vicosa is a pretty white town built on a hillside. Its main praca is overlooked by another dramatic castle - also commissioned by Dom Dinis in the 13th century - its arched entry flanked by massive turrets. It now houses a small archaeological museum. The nearby Church of the Conception has some fine azulejos inside. The Ducal Palace, with a weathered, rose-colored facade of classical design, faces a giant square begun in the 16th century but mostly completed in the 17th. It was built to replace the relatively primitive castle and provide more comfortable and appropriate accommodations for the heirs to the Portuguese throne. The many-chimneyed palace is now a museum and may be visited on guided tours. Adjoining the palace is the Tapada, a 5000-acre park, formerly the royal hunting preserve.

From Vila Vicosa take N255 north to BORBA, another attractive white village.

Both Borba and Vila Vicosa owe their prosperity to the marble of the nearby Montes Claros. The road between the two towns is flanked by marble quarries and mounds of giant marble boulders. As you enter town, watch for the imposing 18th-century fountain sculpted from the pale-pink, locally manufactured marble. You will see it on your right as you reach the main intersection with N4. Turn right on N4 for the remaining 28 kilometers to ELVAS and the POUSADA DE SANTA LUZIA, a simple but satisfying inn whose renowned dining room Spaniards cross the border to frequent. To reach the pousada, stay on the highway toward Spain (ESPANHA) as it circles south of the town proper.

Pousada de Santa Luzia
Elvas

Elvas, only 11 kilometers from the Spanish border, was once the major defensive stronghold in the country. The 16th-century Amoreira Aqueduct, built on Roman foundations, is the most obvious monument in town. It is claimed to be the largest on the Peninsula and is still used to carry water to the city.

Equally impressive are the town walls. Their elaborate construction, with two walls built in the 13th century and one built in the 17th, attest to the continuing importance of the town. Two forts flank the city on the north and south. The Forte de Nossa Senhora da Graca on the north offers splendid views of the town and countryside, and the Forte de Santa Luzia, on the same side of town as the pousada, is alleged to be the best-preserved 17th-century fort in Portugal.

The walled, medieval old city can be entered through the Porta de Olivenca, just east of the pousada. A street of the same name leads directly to the center of town and the Praca da Republica. Just northeast of here are the Church of Nossa Senhora da Consolacao and the Church of Nossa Senhora da Assuncao. Both have lovely azulejo interiors and good paintings.

Continuing in the same general direction brings up the castle, on the north side of the old town. Originally of Moorish construction, it was remodelled extensively in later centuries. A good view of the entire walled city is obtained from here. The rewarding walk around all of the old town is less than three miles and will give you a good idea of the extent of the fortifications.

The narrow cobblestoned streets of the old city are lined with enchanting old residences and picturesque cafes and shops, where you might want to pick up a box of Elvas's famous plums.

Exploring the Alentejo

Medieval Monuments

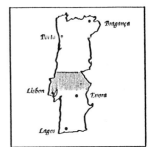

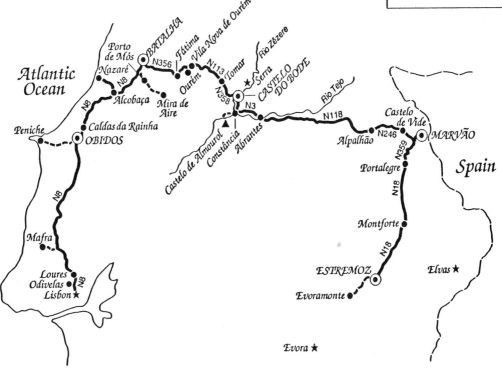

Atlantic Ocean

Spain

79

Medieval Monuments

This itinerary will route you to a number of the most notable medieval monuments in Portugal. It begins with a tour of the ancient region known as Estremadura, which comes from the Latin for "beyond the Douro River," now comprised of only the strip between the Tagus and the sea generally north of Lisbon. This was one of the earliest areas wrested from the Moors in the 12th century, and boasts some of the most well-preserved historic sights in Portugal.

Next the itinerary turns inland and crosses the fertile country known as "Ribatejo," meaning the banks of the Tagus River, where farming and cattle-raising are the primary industries. It winds up in the Upper Alentejo. Alentejo means "beyond the Tagus," which makes sense when you realize these regions were named by the Christians as they made their way down from the north. This area

Tomar
Knights of the Holy Cross Convent

was of particular importance in the 13th and 14th centuries because, once recaptured, it formed the border between the Portuguese kingdom and the Moors to the south and between the Portuguese and the most accessible route from Spain to the east.

Following this route will acquaint you with the diversity of the Portuguese landscape as you encounter a wide variety of food and local handicrafts, and see an equally wide variety of architectural styles, including some of Portugal's most famous tourist attractions.

ORIGINATING CITY   LISBON

Before or after a visit to Lisbon, you'll want to make your way into the interior, where the rhythm and structure of everyday life in the mainly agricultural villages will impart a strong sense of how life has always been lived in Portugal's countryside.

DESTINATION I   OBIDOS   Estalagem do Convento

Leave Lisbon on N8 heading northwest.   Shortly after leaving the city, you'll see a turnoff for ODIVELAS to the left.   A two-kilometer detour will bring you to the little town where the famous King Dom Dinis founded a convent and church in the late 13th century in which he was later buried.

Dom Dinis is one of Portugal's most revered kings.   Previous monarchs had been almost exclusively occupied with the reconquest of Portuguese territory from the Moors (finally achieved in the mid-13th century). During his reign (1279-1325), Dom Dinis oversaw the internal development of the Portuguese economy by promoting agriculture (thus gaining the nickname "O Lavrador," or the farmer) as well as numerous other economic development projects throughout his kingdom. He also established a thriving trade with the rest of Europe which put Portugal in the forefront of seafaring nations. The first university was established under his rule, and a treaty of peace was signed with England in 1308 which is now the oldest existing treaty in the world. He also proclaimed Portuguese - so-called because it was a dialect spoken in the Porto area - as the national language. Finally, he secured a definitive agreement on the exact border between Castile and Portugal, thus assuring the country's independence. He is generally regarded as the father of modern Portugal and you will see evidence of his works all around the country.

Return to N8 and turn left. Continue past VENDA DO PINHEIRO until you come to the intersection with N116 where you turn left for the 10-kilometer drive to MAFRA, a small village which is home to one of Portugal's most impressive national monuments: a 40,000-square-meter palace/monastery. Built in the 18th century by King Joao V, it is (not accidentally) reminiscent of the 16th-century Escorial in Spain, being intentionally designed to surpass it in grandeur. It took some 50,000 workers 13 years to complete (1717-1730).

The Basilica occupies the center of the 800-foot facade and is impressive in its proportions. The vestibule contains a number of huge marble statues of saints. The palace and the monastery are visited (except Tuesdays) by guided tours which take you through the 90 rooms and apartments. Especially noteworthy is the baroque library housing 36,000 volumes, as well as religious manuscripts on parchment. Behind the building is the Tapada Nacional, a national park encircled by a 12-mile-long wall, which was originally the royal hunting grounds. The entire complex is a monument to the power of the Portuguese throne in its heyday, when Brazilian gold flowed into the national coffers.

Estalagem do Convento
Obidos

After you have toured the palace, continue on N116 west to ERICEIRA, a small fishing port with a nice beach where you might like to stop and enjoy the view from one of the numerous outdoor cafes that overlook the water. Then head north on N247, a lovely drive along the ocean to TORRES VEDRAS, an ancient town on the Sizandro River, famous for its wine. If time permits, you can visit its ruined Moorish castle which offers pretty views of the surrounding countryside. Military history buffs will recognize this town as the place where British General Wellington established his lines of defense when the British were helping Portugal against Napoleon.

From Torres Vedras take N8 north to OBIDOS, your destination for tonight and one of Portugal's most picturesque white towns, encircled by walls stretching across a grassy-green hillside. The ESTALAGEM DO CONVENTO is a lovely little inn whose exterior fits in perfectly with its medieval surroundings but which provides modern comforts within.

Obidos's most obvious attraction is the castle looming above town and the extensive, well-preserved, 12th-century fortifications which surround the old section. The castle was originally built by Dom Dinis in the 13th century, then mostly destroyed by the 1755 earthquake and later restored. There is a pousada now occupying part of it (see the hotel descriptions), and there are superb views of the countryside from the castle ramparts.

King Dinis's queen, known as Santa Isabel, admired the town so much that he gave it to her. For the next five centuries the town was considered a possession of the ruling queen.

The ancient, narrow streets are another of its chief attractions. Filled with handicraft shops (lace, leather, baskets, ceramics), the flower-bedecked buildings are charming to see and to explore. The Rua Direita is the main street which leads from the handsome main gate to the castle, passing the market square and the most interesting church, Saint Mary's. Next door is the museum, with a collection of religious art and a room with antique arms and a model of the Lines of Torres Vedras. The town is made for leisurely wandering and picture-taking of enchanting nooks and crannies off cobblestone streets overshadowed by dazzling-white houses with iron balconies and colorfully painted doors.

An interesting sidetrip from Obidos is to seaside PENICHE, 25 kilometers west on N114. Squat, white windmills are characteristic of this area of the country, and you'll see several along the way, but few are still in use. However, just before you get to Peniche, you'll find on your right a working example, now home to a curio shop where windmill replicas in all sizes are sold. Peniche is an active, rambling old fishing port with a large harbor, surrounded by grassy sand dunes. A bit beyond is CARVOEIRO CAPE whose oddly shaped rock formations attest to the relentless assault of the sea. In the midsummer months an hour-long boat trip goes to the BERLENGAS ISLANDS off Peniche (look for the signs for Berlengas in the harbor area). The main island has a 17th-century fort and some great hiking paths, but just the boat ride itself makes a fun trip.

Leave Obidos heading north on N8 to CALDAS DA RAINHA (the Spa of the Queen), founded in the 15th century by Queen Leonor, wife of Joao II. The Dom Carlos I Park is on the right as you enter town. In the middle of the park is the Museu de Jose Malhoa with a collection of modern Portuguese painting and ceramics. At the north end of the park is a statue of the queen and, if you turn right here, you'll soon come across the Manueline church, Nossa Senhora do Populo, its interior colorfully adorned with azulejos. Next to it is the bathhouse founded by the queen in 1504, which is still in use. If you happen to be here on Monday, it's worth walking north a couple of blocks to see the lively market in the main square.

Continue on N8 to ALCOBACA, which derives its name from its situation on the confluence of the Alcoa and Baca rivers. It is also the home of the Real Abadia de Santa Maria de Alcobaca, one of Portugal's most outstanding monuments, which dominates the center of town. Founded in 1178 by Portugal's first king, Dom Afonso Henriques, the Cistercian monastery is a marvel of medieval architecture. The church is impressive for its extreme length compared to its narrow width. In the transept of the church are the intricately carved limestone tombs of Ines de Castro (on the left) and King Pedro I, whose tragic love story has set the theme for numerous literary works.

Ines, a lady-in-waiting to Prince Pedro's wife, proved irresistibly attractive to the young prince and, when his wife died, he installed Ines as his mistress, since her humble origins forbade her marriage to the future king. Although their love was idyllic, many of the nobles feared that the illegitimate offspring of this union would aspire to the throne. They convinced the king, Afonso IV, to condone her murder. When Afonso died and Pedro became king, he set out to avenge her death by hunting down and punishing the noble murderers one by one.

Legend has it (probably fictitiously) that Pedro exhumed the skeleton of his dead paramour, had her crowned queen in regal dress and forced the nobility to file by and kiss her hand. At any rate, he did spend much time and energy during his short reign (1357-1367) exalting her memory and, as you can see, provided quite handsomely for their eternal resting places. They are allegedly positioned so that when their souls were resurrected, the first sight of each would be the other.

On the opposite side of the pretty cloister from the church are the abbey buildings, including the impressive kitchen through which flows a branch of the River Alcoa which provided the monks with fish. Next to it is the spacious refectory, sometimes used today as a community theater.

Town activity centers around the large main square, its numerous shops proffering a wide variety of the distinctive blue-and-white ceramic typical of the area.

Leave Alcobaca on N8 heading north, passing through ALJUBARROTA, the little town that gave its name to one of the most famous battles in Portuguese

Pousada do Mestre Afonso Domingues
Batalha

Medieval Monuments

history, but which is otherwise of little interest. The battle was fought in 1385 between the Portuguese and the Castilians, and the victory of the former, despite being outnumbered three to one, assured the nation's independence for the next two centuries.

Only 15 kilometers now separate you from BATALHA, your destination for tonight. If time permits, consider a five-kilometer detour to the ancient town of PORTO DE MOS (turn right at CRUZ DA LEGUA). It has a fabulous castle which sits on an isolated hill overlooking the Lena River. The handsome lines of the small fortified castle lend it a distinctly French appearance. It was originally built as a fortress in the 9th century, but was remodelled in the 15th for use as a palace. It has been recently restored by the National Agency for Historical Monuments. Unique green tiles on the towers shimmer in the sun, creating a striking vision.

The POUSADA DO MESTRE AFONSO DOMINGUES is located in Batalha, in the shadow of a monastery of even grander proportions than the one in Alcobaca. The inn is named for the principal architect of the Mosteiro de Maria da Vitoria, dedicated to Our Lady of Victory and built by Joao I to commemorate, and give thanks for, the victory of the Portuguese at Aljubarrota.

The monastery is a combination of Gothic and Manueline styles. Tall stained-glass windows are the first and only thing you notice upon entering (until your eyes adjust to the interior dimness). To the immediate right is the stark, white Founder's Chapel sheltering the tomb of Joao I and his English wife, Philippa of Lancaster (in the center). Other notables rest in carved niches around the walls, including Joao's son, Henry the Navigator, founder of the school of navigation at Sagres which made possible the great voyages of discovery in the 15th and 16th centuries (although Henry himself never went).

On the left, across the nave, is the entrance to the Royal Cloister whose delightful garden patio is overlooked through graceful, carved Gothic arcades -

almost no two alike. To the right as you enter is the Chapter House which contains the Tomb of the Unknown Soldier from World War I, where two modern-day soldiers keep vigil. Actually there are two unknown soldiers, too, one who died in Europe and one who died in Africa, along with an eternal flame fueled by pure Portuguese olive oil. The former refectory on the opposite side of the cloister houses a Museum of the Unknown Soldier featuring the tributes paid by foreign dignitaries upon visiting the tomb.

Beyond, and in sharp contrast to, the Royal Cloister is the plainly severe Cloister of Dom Afonso V, added later. From here you exit and walk to the right around the outside to reach the dramatic unfinished chapels (Capelas Imperfeitas), built in rich Manueline style to be King Duarte's chapel. Both his tomb and his wife's are there, but the chapel not entirely - massive, ornately carved buttresses climb to the open sky, patiently awaiting the weight of a roof which was never completed. .

As in Alcobaca, shops and cafes are found in the immediate vicinity of the monastery and, beyond that, the town features some pretty 17th- and 18th-century houses and a nice parish church.

An interesting sidetrip from Batalha, especially for armchair spelunkers, is to head south through PORTO DE MOS, with its splendid castle, and then southeast on N243 toward MIRA DE AIRE, an important textile area. There are four caves you can visit: the GRUTAS DE ALVADOS, with a series of interesting chambers; the nearby GRUTAS DE SANTO ANTONIO, some 6000 square meters in area (both of these are reached before Mira de Aire); the GRUTAS MIRA DE AIRE, supposedly the deepest in Europe; and, north of Mira de Aire near SAO MAMEDE, the GRUTAS DE MOEDA, smaller and at a depth of 45 meters. If you are only casually interested in caves, the second and third are the most interesting.

Leave Batalha heading east on N356 toward Fatima.   Just beyond REGUENGOS DO FETAL are good views back over the ground you just covered, its green hills dotted with windmills.   Another 10 kilometers brings you to COVA DE IRIA and FATIMA which, like Lourdes in France, is a pilgrimage center of international renown (follow the signs reading "SANTUARIO").   Legend has it that the Virgin appeared to three shepherd children - Lucia, Francisco and Jacinta - on May 13, 1917, and on the 13th of each month thereafter until October, bearing a message of peace.   The spot began to draw religious pilgrims almost immediately, although the immense neoclassical Basilica, enveloped by a 40-acre park, was not constructed until the 1950s.   Popes Paul VI and John Paul II have both visited here.   A small chapel marks the spot where the apparition occurred and, at almost any hour, you will witness the faithful on their knees, traversing the broad esplanade which fronts it.   On the 13th of each month from May to October, in accordance with the legend, attendance multiplies and includes a torchlight procession at night.

Continue north for 11 kilometers, join N133 and turn left to the town of VILA NOVA DE OUREM.   You're bound to notice the picturesque fortified town crowning a hill overlooking Vila Nova.   This is the ancient town of OUREM, today virtually abandoned, which is reached up a steep, winding road.   The original castle was turned into a palace by the Count of Ourem in the 15th century.   Leave your car just inside the walled entrance and walk around the charming, lonely village and up to the castle.   The visit imparts an almost eerie feel for life in the distant past.   The vistas from the belvedere over the green countryside are striking.

Descend to Vila Nova and continue east on N113 another 20 kilometers to TOMAR, one of the oldest cities in Portugal.   The site was originally awarded

Pousada de Sao Pedro
Tomar-Castelo de Bode

to the Knights Templar when they were persuaded by Afonso Henriques, Portugal's first king, to help fight the Moors in the 12th century. When they were subsequently disbanded by the Pope, King Dinis created the Order of the Knights of Christ to replace them, and the new order appropriated the castle as their headquarters. The wealth of this new order, always close to the royal family, was later to facilitate the great age of discovery. Henry the Navigator was its Grand Master during much of the 15th century, and the order sponsored numerous exploratory voyages along the coast of Africa, its holdings there and in the East Indies making it the richest knightly order in Christendom. Times changed however and, in the early 16th century, the order became monastic.

The old Templar castle walls surround the convent inside. Be sure to allow enough time to investigate fully the elaborate complex and its multiple cloisters. The Templar church, called the rotunda, has 16 sides, in imitation of the Church of the Holy Sepulchre in Jerusalem. Two stellar examples of Manueline-style architecture are found here in the entrance and window of the church, both painstakingly and ornately carved. Manueline decorative motifs, as you'll note here, emphasized marine elements as well as natural ones, such as trees, masts, ropes, anchor chains, etc.

The town of Tomar occupies an appealing spot on the bank of the Nabao River. There is an unusually pretty riverside park with a lovely waterfall along the edge of the placid river as it flows through the center of town. Besides its enchanting setting, and as you might suspect, other notable sights in town consist mainly of churches and chapels.

To arrive at tonight's destination, take N110 south, watching for signs directing you to follow N358 to the CASTELO DE BODE dam and the sleepy POUSADA DE SAO PEDRO, overlooking the deep-blue water of the reservoir and the Zezere River.

DESTINATION IV   MARVAO   Pda. de Santa Maria

Today's drive takes you across Portugal almost to the Spanish border, and into the beautiful mountain country of the SERRA DE MARVAO and the SERRA DE SAO MAMEDE. Continue south on the road fronting the pousada for an arduous but scenic drive to CONSTANCIA, at the confluence of the Zezere and Tagus rivers. If you detour briefly southwest on N3 you will be rewarded with the breathtaking sight of 12th-century Almourol castle perched dramatically atop a rocky island in the middle of the Tagus. It was built by the Templars before they went to Tomar. From the riverbank you can usually hire a boat to circle the island.

Return to N3 and head east, back through Constancia and on to ABRANTES, an old-world town dominated by castle ruins which afford good views from the restored keep, and some remaining fortifications. Go through town and follow the signs for PORTALEGRE, leaving town on N118. Another 25 kilometers bring you to GAVIAO, an agricultural town in an area of extensive cultivation. The boulder-strewn landscape tells a tale of toil for the local farmers, and reveals the source for the hand-constructed rock walls lining the road. Approximately 30 kilometers more bring you to the foot of the Serra de Sao Mamede at ALPALHAO, where you commence the climb toward CASTELO DE VIDE on N246.

Castelo de Vide offers a charming reminder of the distant past. Tiny cobblestone lanes, often stepped, run between barely separated buildings constructed in a time when nothing larger than a horse had to pass between them. At the foot of the castle is the Judaria, or Jewish Quarter, which will reward a short stroll with glimpses of the past through the doors and windows. Walk up to the Sao Roque Fort for some excellent views of the town and surrounding countryside.

Leave town on N246-1 in the direction of MÀRVAO. You traverse a tree-lined country road flanked by pasture land and olive groves as you ascend the Serra. Start watching for signs to the unpretentious but welcoming POUSADA DE SANTA MARIA, which you reach along a winding road with extensive panoramas. The hilltop town of Marvao rises more than 2,500 feet above sea level and is visible up to the right upon your approach. As romantic as its setting appears today, from its massive and apparently impregnable fortifications it's plain to see why, historically, unwelcome aggressors would consider this strategic position next to impossible to overcome.

This picturesque little mountain town is completely ringed by the imposing ramparts of its 13th-century castle, another of King Dinis's defensive installations against the ever-suspect Spaniards (it was previously also a Roman stronghold called Herminio Minor). The narrow streets betray the town's age and, along with a profusion of wrought-iron windows and flowery balconies on whitewashed houses, paint an authentic and charming picture of life here as it has been for centuries. Meander through the quaint village up to the castle ramparts, which you can stroll around for glorious views over red rooftops to the Serra stretching for miles beyond. Another worthwhile visit is to the pretty little church of Nossa Senhora da Estrela.

Pousada de Santa Maria
Marvao

DESTINATION V   ESTREMOZ   Pda. Rainha Santa Isabel

Though few spots are sufficiently isolated to match the atmosphere of the one you are departing, today's destination is still considered one of Portugal's most historically appealing towns.

After descending the hill to the main road, continue straight ahead on N359 through rocky terrain only occasionally interrupted by signs of habitation, to PORTALEGRE, a commercial city dominated by its cathedral. For a dramatic and elevated view of the town as well as the surrounding mountain scenery, take N246-2 to the left on the southern edge of town and, after about eight kilometers, take a small road to the right. After a couple of kilometers bear left to the highest peak in the area, Sao Mamede (3500 feet). You'll get captivating glimpses of Portalegre, with its cathedral spires jutting against the sky, as you make your way down.

From Portalegre head south on N18. The tree-lined country lane runs through cultivated, green countryside, sprinkled with cattle, olive trees and cork oaks. The farming town of MONFORTE seems to doze contentedly in the shadow of its ruined 14th-century castle. You'll bypass numerous sleepy, rural villages en route to your destination, ESTREMOZ, where signs lead you faithfully to one of Portugal's most outstanding pousadas, the RAINHA SANTA ISABEL. Installed in a 14th-century royal palace, once the residence of King Dom Dinis I and his queen Isabel, it offers sumptuous lodgings for modern-day travellers.

The major attractions of Estremoz are its picturesque setting and Moorish character. The medieval atmosphere has been largely retained in the narrow lanes and historic buildings, both employing the local white marble in their construction. This is most apparent in the area around the pousada, situated in the upper town. You will especially want to explore the neighborhood around the Largo do Castelo Square and see the Chapel of the Saint Queen with its lovely azulejo interior. Queen Isabel, wife of Dom Dinis, died here in 1336 after an arduous journey, and the painted tiles depict the various miracles attributed to her life's work spent in the service of the poor. She was beloved of the Portuguese people and was canonized in the 16th century.

The 13th-century, 100-foot keep flanking the pousada is called the "Tower of Three Crowns" because its construction spanned the reigns of three monarchs. There are fabulous views from its battlements. Nearby is the Church of St. Mary which dates from the 16th century.

Pousada Rainha Santa Isabel
Estremoz

Estremoz has always been famous for its ceramics, both functional and decorative. If you walk from the pousada down to the lower town (centered around the main Praca do Marques de Pombal), you will encounter numerous outlets for it.   On the way you will pass the Luis de Camoes Square, its marble pillory silent testimony to the trials of the Inquisition.   On the south side of the main square is the 17th-century town hall, now housing the municipal museum, which has a good collection of popular art, as well as ethnographic and archaeological exhibits.

If you are fortunate or foresighted enough to be here on a Saturday, you can enjoy a lively market in and around the main square displaying everything from handicrafts, ceramics and marble, to livestock, clothing and old furniture.

Port to Port

Matosinhos
PORTO

A1

Murtosa
Cacia
AVEIRO

Albergaria-a-Velha
Oliveira
São Pedro do Sul
N16
N16 Viseu
Mangualde
N232
Nelas
Gouveia
Luso
Mortágua
N231 N17 MANTEIGAS
Mealhada
BUÇACO
N234
Sta. Gomba Dão
Torre
Canas de Senhorim

N1

Atlantic Ocean

Coimbra
Condeixa
▲ Conímbriga

Pombal

N8 N1
Leiria
Batalha

SÃO MARTINHO
DO PORTO
Alcobaça
Caldas da Rainha
Obidos
Rio Maior

★ Castelo do Bode

N1

Vila Franca de Xira

N10

★ Lisbon

★ Palmela
Azeitão ★ Setúbal

Porto
Bragança
Lisbon
Evora
Lagos

97

Port to Port

This itinerary takes you along the Atlantic shore of Portugal from Lisbon, the country's most important port, to Porto, the second in importance. You will often see Porto spelled Oporto, especially in the United Kingdom. That is simply a variant retaining the article "o" which means "the." Oporto simply means "the port." Porto is the Portuguese form, though, so we'll be using that. That word is also the source of the word Portuguese, as it was the Porto dialect that King Dinis proclaimed to be the national language in the 13th century.

The itinerary follows the coastline known as the Costa de Prata (the silver coast). This is one of the less-developed coasts and rather less spoiled by modern highrises, quaint fishing villages with pretty beaches being more the rule than the exception.

Nazare

The trip is not all seacoast, however, since we detour inland to visit three of the country's most compelling sights: the romantic forest of Bucaco, the old university city of Coimbra, and the spectacular mountain scenery of the Serra da Estrela, Portugal's highest range.

We wind up in Portugal's second city, Porto, situated at the mouth of the Douro River, second in size only to the Tagus. Although considerably smaller than Lisbon, Porto is a very cosmopolitan city with strong historical and commercial bonds with Britain. Here the British discovered, and acquired a taste for, the local wine known as Port, and it has been big business ever since.

ORIGINATING CITY   LISBON

Sophisticated Lisbon is fun to visit, but the rest of the country has attractions to offer with which the capital city cannot compete. This itinerary should paint some new colors into your picture of Portugal.

DESTINATION I   SAO MARTINHO DO PORTO   Hotel Parque

Your first destination is a picturesque little fishing port on a protected bay. Leave Lisbon on the freeway N1, following it to its termination near AVEIRAS DE CIMA about 52 kilometers northeast. As you zoom along you will skirt the edge of the inland estuary of the Tagus with port facilities and a number of small industrial towns. At VILA FRANCA DE XIRA you will see an almost mile-long bridge spanning the river which, until the 1960s, was the only bridge near Lisbon. When the freeway peters out, bear left on N366 and continue for 42 kilometers through primarily agricultural land to CALDAS DA RAINHA, formerly the mineral baths of Queen Leonor, wife of Joao II, called "the Perfect Prince" and generally considered Portugal's greatest monarch (1481-1495). At the rear of the large park to the left as you enter town is the interesting Igreja (Church) do Populo, and a few blocks north of there is the main square which is especially colorful on market day (Monday).

Hotel Parque
Sao Martinho do Porto

Leave Caldas heading north on N8 and continue for a pretty 12 kilometers to the left turnoff for ALFEIZERAO. Just a few more kilometers bring you to tonight's destination, SAO MARTINHO DO PORTO and the old-world HOTEL PARQUE, situated only a couple of blocks from the half-moon beach of this tiny fishing port.

Sao Martinho is on a conch-shell-shaped bay edged with sandy dunes and sheltered by rocky cliffs. The calm water is dotted with colorful, bobbing fishing boats. (This is a particularly good beach if you happen to be travelling with children.) Don't miss the panorama from the Monte Facho viewpoint at the north end of the beach or the opportunity to indulge in the local specialty, lobster, along the waterfront. Otherwise you need feel compelled to do nothing but relax in this tranquil spot.

While staying in Sao Martinho, you should plan to make an excursion to the neighboring fishing village of NAZARE (12 kilometers north on N242). This is the coast's best-known tourist attraction, especially in the summer when native costumes add to the local color. At the extreme north end of the Nazare beach looms the promontory called Sitio. You can ride the funicular up from the lower (Praia) area, or you can take N242 toward MARINHA GRANDE and turn left when you get to the top of the hill. The Sitio is worth a visit if only for the panoramic views from the belvedere. While you're there, stop in to see the colorful azulejos in the church nearby.

The main hub of activity is the Praia area down below. Souvenir and handicraft shops line the north end of the beachfront, which they share with a myriad of small restaurants featuring an endless variety of seafood, logically enough. We enjoyed picking out our lobster and crab (billed by weight) at the RESTAURANTE MAR E SOL. Street vendors offering everything from model boats to sardines drying on wire racks complete the picture of a bustling resort town. Away from the beach you'll encounter a labyrinth of narrow winding streets crowded with mostly residential buildings.

Down the beach at the end of the day you can see the town's age-old livelihood carried out as dark-clad fishermen in long caps haul in their day's catch. Since Nazare lacks a real harbor, the fishermen pull their colorfully painted boats from the water onto the beach (traditionally by oxen, now more often by tractors) for safekeeping overnight. Conveniently located across the street is the fish market which makes for an interesting, if malodorous, visit.

Today's destination is a change of pace - no beach, no fishing village - being instead in the heart of a magnificent, unspoiled forest.

Take N242 north, bypassing Nazare (if you didn't see it while staying in Sao Martinho, you could stop for a quick visit today), and continue to MARINHA GRANDE. You pass along the Leiria pine forest planted by King Dinis in the 13th century to retard erosion of the sand. Marinha Grande is an industrial town which owes its origin to the Stephens brothers from England who founded a glass factory here in the 18th century. It is currently the center of glass and crystal production in Portugal.

Bear right, still on N242, to LEIRIA, dominated by an imposing 12th-century castle. Rising majestically over the town, it affords wonderful views, particularly from the keep. Inside the castle is Our Lady of Sorrow Church, built in the 14th century in early Gothic style. The well-preserved Royal Palace, once the residence of Dom Dinis and his wife, St. Isabel, is also within.

From Leiria take N1, the major north-south highway, north toward POMBAL and COIMBRA. The former sits in the shadow of its castle and is named for the Marques de Pombal, minister of King Jose in the 18th century. The King was uninterested in affairs of state and left Pombal in charge. The Marques assumed his responsibilities with a vengeance and ruled as an enlightened despot in the 18th-century fashion. Though many of his policies were revoked by Queen Maria I, who succeeded Jose, his economic policies were generally retained and, since he was in power after the earthquake of 1755, he is responsible for the reconstruction and design of many areas which were affected. He died here after being dismissed from his duties and, if you go into town, you will see a memorial dedicated to him in the main square.

The small castle is one of many built in the 12th century by Gualdim Pais, Grand Master of the Order of the Knights Templar during the campaign against the Moors. It is relatively well-preserved atop its wooded hill overlooking the town.

Another 29 kilometers will bring you to CONDEIXA. If you follow the signs for N3422 and CONIMBRIGA, you will arrive shortly at one of the most impressive Roman ruins on the Peninsula, dating from the 1st to the 3rd centuries A.D. On the right after entering is a beautifully preserved mosaic floor edged by gardens. Actually once the interior patio of a large house (called the House of Fountains), it is surrounded by dozens of tiny, arching water spouts. Originally driven solely by gravity, they now operate when the attendant starts an underground pump, which he will do for demonstration purposes (though you may have to ask). Numerous other interesting unearthings - skeletons, baths, pools, an aqueduct - are to be found at the site.

If you return to the road and go right, you come upon the surprisingly modern museum containing the artifacts (jewelry, glass, bronze, ceramics, sculpture, etc.) discovered in the excavation. There is also a small shop where some rather nice replicas are sold.

Return to Condeixa and head north. Watch for signs leading to the A1 freeway, a stretch just long enough to avoid the city congestion. Exit when it ends and head east to MEALHADA. Continue east on N234 in the direction of LUSO and VISEU. In Luso watch for signs at a right turnoff for your destination, BUCACO, and the magnificent PALACE HOTEL DO BUCACO. The elaborate hotel is reminiscent of a grand English country estate, situated in the awesome Bucaco National Park at an altitude of about 1200 feet above sea level.

Long a protected area, the Bucaco Forest was taken over by the Discalced Carmelites in the 17th century. The meditative order added to the number of distinct species of flora during their residence and constructed a continuous wall around the area. A papal bull in 1643 forbade the cutting of the trees and threatened excommunication for those who did.

Bucaco was the scene of an important battle between General Wellington and the Napoleonic invaders in 1810. Wellington and a combined British and Portuguese contingent occupied the high ground and won the encounter. The French were forced to retreat and had to console themselves with the sacking of Coimbra. Wellington and his troops retired to the area defended by the lines of Torres Vedras.

In 1834 all church property was secularized and the forest passed to the state, when even more species of trees were planted until today the total exceeds 600 specimens from around the world.

In the late 19th century a summer palace was built for the royal family. When the Republic was proclaimed in 1910, the royal family quietly left the country and the palace was converted into a private hotel (though the government owns the building), one of Portugal's most magnificent, and a remarkable place to stay while you explore the site's natural beauty.

Numerous marked trails leave the hotel in all directions, taking you through the dense forest to the viewpoints, tiny hermitages, springs and pools which dot the area. The "Via Sacra," or Way of the Cross path, twists up to the highest peak, the Cruz Alta, which has spellbinding views of the surrounding area and of several other mountain ranges. This peak may also be reached by road if you aren't up for a three-hour hike, and there are other appealing points which require less effort.

The very lively old university city of COIMBRA deserves an all-day visit, but its hotel offerings are not as attractive as the town. Word is that a pousada is being built there, but not before 1988 or so. We recommend, therefore, that you stay in the wonderful Hotel Palace and spend a day in Coimbra from there. From LUSO take N235 south for a beautiful, though mountainous and winding, drive to

Palace Hotel do Bucaco
Bucaco

PENACOVA, a pretty little town hanging balcony-like over the Mondego River valley and affording excellent views from the center of the village. The town is famous for its hand-carved willow-wood toothpicks. A few kilometers beyond Penacova on N110 watch for a turnoff to the right for a short, wooded drive to LORVAO, site of a monastery founded in the 6th century, one of the oldest on the Peninsula. It was later turned into a convent and the daughters of Sancho I (1185-1211) were interred there. The actual convent was extensively remodelled in the 18th century and is now a hospital. The silver shrines of the two ladies are now in the main chapel of the interesting 16th-century church.

Return to N110 and turn right for the remaining 24 kilometers to Coimbra. One of Portugal's most tradition-laden cities, Coimbra deserves the kind of attention to detail which can be had only by walking the ancient streets and alleyways.

Coimbra was, from the 12th to the 13th centuries, the capital of Portugal. The first Portuguese university was established here in the 14th century, but was moved to Lisbon for a time. It was permanently returned to this city in 1537, and Coimbra has been the intellectual center of the country, indeed, of the whole Portuguese Empire, ever since.

The older town on the hill is the location of the majority of the sights. The original university buildings are here, alongside some rather prosaic newer structures. Retaining the old ways, some students can still be seen in traditional black capes bearing colorful ribbons corresponding to their faculty (medicine, law, etc.). The main university building has a large central patio, and the impressive library building is just outside.

Just down the hill to the north you will find the Machado de Castro Museum with admirable collections of painting, sculpture, ceramics and furniture, as well as a display of Roman antiquities.

Slightly behind the museum is the old cathedral (Se Velha), a good example of the Romanesque style from the 12th century and containing a fine Gothic retable in the soaring interior.

A long walk down the hill past the old cathedral passes through the old part of the city, then the notable Almedina Gate and, beyond that, the lower town (the more modern part) along the Rua Ferreira Borges (on the north it becomes Visconde) where the main shopping area is. At the north end of the street is the Monastery of Santa Cruz (on the 8th of May Square), in whose church is the impressive tomb, among others, of Afonso Henriques, the first King of Portugal. A bit to the east of the monastery is the large, colorful central market, worth a short visit.

If you are travelling with children, you might enjoy a visit to the children's park called "Portugal dos Pequeninos," (Children's Portugal), a complex of miniature buildings representing the geographical styles of the whole country and of the former overseas empire. It is located across the Santa Clara Bridge over the Mondego River: if you follow the signs for Lisboa, they will take you across the bridge. Just after crossing, N1 turns left and you continue straight ahead. In this same area is the Santa Clara-a-Nova Convent where the remains of the Saint Queen Isabel (wife of King Dinis) lie in a silver tomb.

You can return to Bucaco the way you came, or, if you've lingered too long in charming Coimbra, you can take N1 to Mealhada and N234 to Luso for a quicker trip.

DESTINATION III   MANTEIGAS   Pda. de Sao Lourenco

Although Bucaco and the Hotel Palace are difficult to leave behind, the next destination will provide a very different, but delightful stopping place in the Serra da Estrela, Portugal's highest mountain range. Leave Bucaco heading east on N234, bypassing MORTAGUA after 13 kilometers. Another few kilometers, through gorgeous landscape, brings you to SANTA COMBA DAO. Just beyond the town bear right (the signs say GUARDA and CARREGAL) through the little town of VIMEIRO, the birth- and final resting place of Antonio Oliveira Salazar, dictator of Portugal from 1932 to 1968. Just beyond town take a left on N234, where you'll be greeted by a succession of tidy towns surrounded by olive groves and the vineyards which produce Dao wine.

After 26 kilometers you will reach the quaint old town of CANAS DE SENHORIM, crowded with stone-block houses with wooden or stone balconies. Soon thereafter is the little town of NELAS, where you turn right on N231. The snow-capped peaks of the Serra da Estrela now lie on the horizon and, after 21 kilometers and a crossing of the Mondego River, you will reach SEIA, a charmingly situated market town at the foot of the mountains. Bear left toward GOUVEIA through a number of picturesque hamlets and some extraordinary scenery. Also along this road are a number of "artesanato" (handicraft) stores specializing in leather goods (vests, jackets, fur-lined slippers, purses, etc.).

From Gouveia take N232 toward MANTEIGAS. This is a tortuously winding mountain road and requires a careful approach, but it also has some remarkable views of the Serra. Part-way up is a sign saying "Cabeca do Velho" (old man's head) and if you look to your right, following the arrow, you'll notice a rock outcropping resembling the title given it. Watch also for a sign indicating the "Nascente do Mondego," or the origin of the Mondego River, which flows east from here, then curls back west in a much larger form. Another 20 kilometers along this dramatic road brings you to POUSADA DE SAO LOURENCO, perched high above the River Zezere with truly impressive views of Manteigas in the valley below and of TORRE, Portugal's highest peak at 6500 feet.

While in this scenic area don't fail to descend the switchbacked mountain road to the colorful town of Manteigas, set like a jewel amid one of the most striking

Pousada de Sao Lourenco
Manteigas

settings imaginable. It's situated at the head of a narrow valley surrounded on all sides by terraced farms stairstepping their way up the steep hillsides. Just west of town, as you enter the valley, a six-kilometer detour to the left leads to the Poco do Inferno (the Well of Hell) where a waterfall flows wildly into a deep cave.

If time permits, the 70-kilometer round-trip excursion to the top of Torre Peak beyond Manteigas will guarantee unparalleled panoramas. (In winter the road is often closed by snow - ask at the pousada first, in that case.) Along the way you pass through the unusual-looking, boulder-strewn glacial valley where the River Zezere is born.

Above all the whole area is perfect for picnicking, exploring and soaking up the gorgeous surrounding landscape before returning to relax in cozy comfort in the pousada.

DESTINATION IV   AVEIRO   Hotel Paloma Blanca

Today you head back to the coast, to the northern end of the Costa de Prata where generally cooler weather prevails due to the ocean currents.

Wind your way back down to Gouveia toward MANGUALDE on N232. Notice the broadened Mondego as you cross. Join N16 leaving town to the north, and another 15 kilometers brings you to the beautiful old red-roofed town of VISEU, clustered around its cathedral on the banks of the Pavia River. You get a splendid view as you approach.

Center of a 16th-century school of painting, Viseu boasts a good art museum: the Museu Grao Vasco. "O Grao Vasco," the great Basque (Fernandes), was one of the founders of the school. The museum is housed in a 16th-century mansion and located on the large cathedral square in the center of the old town. The 13th-century (subsequently remodelled) cathedral with its Manueline vault is worth a visit, too. Stroll around the enchanting old town to see the impressive mansions dating from the 16th, 17th and 18th centuries.

Continue on N16 through pretty countryside to SAO PEDRO DO SUL, near a mineral spa whose waters will cure, they say, almost anything that ails you. This is one of the most picturesque villages in the region, situated at the confluence of the Sul and Vouga Rivers and surrounded by deep green, terraced hillsides.

Bear left, remaining on N16, to VOUZELA. As you enter, note on your right the enchanting little church, its facade totally covered with blue-and-white tiles. In this area you begin to encounter "espigueiros," the characteristic storage and smoking sheds set on stilts next to the stone houses or in the fields. They are typical of northern Portugal and Galicia in Spain (where they are called "horreos").

Stay on N16, passing through the heavily cultivated northern countryside and OLIVEIRA DO FRADES to PESSEGUEIRO, where you cross the Vouga River. Another 15 kilometers brings you to ALBERGARIA-A-VELHA, where you jog north a bit, then bear left for the last 21 kilometers to AVEIRO, your destination for today. Your simply appointed, but charming hotel in Aveiro, the PALOMA BLANCA, is centrally located and will allow you to explore much of the picturesque city on foot.

The most notable feature of Aveiro is its large lagoon, formed by a long, thin sandbar, some 30 miles long and one-and-a-half miles across at its widest. The average depth, outside the canals the ships use, is only a little over six feet. The numerous canals crisscrossing the town itself add to its considerable charm.

Hotel Paloma Blanca
Aveiro

Naturally enough, most activity in Aveiro centers around the water. The major products are salt from the surrounding saltpans, seaweed (used for fertilizer), and fish taken from the lagoon. Boat trips around the lagoon are sometimes available, depending on the time of year. They take you near the seashore lined with lovely houses and, although it's a fading practice, with a little luck you'll see the colorful, flat-bottomed boats called "moliceiros" collecting seaweed. Check with the tourist office on the Praca da Republica for current schedules and prices. One tour includes lunch at the Pousada da Ria on the other side of the lagoon (see hotel listings). If you prefer, you could visit the area by driving north on N109 to ESTARREJA, then turning left on N109-5. Here you cross the bridge over the lagoon and join up with N327, where you again turn left for the 20-kilometer trip along the water to SAO JACINTO beach at the tip of the bar. The whole trip will take about an hour each way, not counting stops.

In town there are worthwhile sights, mostly in the area to the south of the central Humberto Delgado Square, which is actually a wide bridge over the main canal.

The art museum, in a former convent, has a good collection of Portuguese art from all periods. The convent itself contains the baroque tomb of Santa Joana, daughter of King Afonso V, who died here in 1490. On the same street is the Misericordia Church which has a striking baroque doorway and extensive azulejo decoration.

There are also several beaches about 10 kilometers south of town - somewhat closer than Sao Jacinto, though less picturesque. Barra and Costa Nova beaches are both on the Atlantic. You will see signs in town pointing the way on N109-7.

As you might expect, seafood is the main gastronomical fare around here. Two local specialties, for the adventurous, are eel stew (caldeirada de enguias) and an egg-based sweet called "ovos moles." Aveiro has also long been a center of fine pottery and porcelain production, and you'll find both for sale around town, but, if you are a true potteryphile, you might want to make the eight-kilometer excursion (south on N109) to a little town called VISTA ALEGRE, world-famous for its pottery works since 1824, which now has a museum depicting the history of developments in pottery manufacture. The porcelain made here is of an extremely fine quality and often hand-painted with a faint oriental flair.

DESTINATION V   PORTO   Hotel Infante de Sagres

Today's drive is a short one, but there is plenty to see once you arrive at your destination. Leave Aveiro heading north on N109 through ESTARREJA and AVANCA, bypassing the little fishing village of OVAR. Another 16 kilometers brings you to the small coastal town of ESPINHO, recently endowed with a casino and converted into a seaside resort. At this point you are officially on the COSTA VERDE (green coast), Portugal's northernmost shores. Espinho has a pretty, palm-lined esplanade which makes a good spot for a break before picking up the freeway for the short drive into PORTO. You approach the city over the Arrabida Bridge, the youngest, longest and westernmost of the three spectacular spans across the Douro River. The one you see to your right is the Dom Luis I, built in 1886, and beyond that is the railway bridge, Maria Pia, built 10 years earlier by Gustave Eiffel (before he built the tower in Paris). As is inevitably the case, the finest city views are available from these vantage points.

Your hotel here, the HOTEL INFANTE DE SAGRES, is downtown, so follow the CENTRO signs to find it. Located on a relatively quiet praca down a side street, it escapes a lot of the noise and traffic normally associated with such a convenient situation. Its namesake, and Porto's native son (1394), is Prince Henry the Navigator, the driving force behind Portugal's monumental voyages of discovery, famous for his school of navigation in Sagres. His parents were King Joao I and Philippa of Lancaster, daughter of John of Gaunt. Their marriage in 1387 cemented the bond that Porto still maintains with the British. In the 18th century the British discovered the wine called "Port," and the rest is history.

Porto is the second largest city in Portugal, with nearly half a million inhabitants, and the heart of the nation's most important economic region, accounting for well over 50% of the country's economic production. The city has a long history of relative autonomy (fiercely protected), and has frequently found itself at odds with Lisbon. Unaffected by the 1755 earthquake, Porto retains an old-world ambiance unmatched in the capital city.

Most of the important sights are reached easily on foot from your hotel. Just a block east is the bustling Avenida dos Aliados which runs from the Town Hall on the north to the busy Liberdade Square (the center of town) on the south. A few blocks to the west of the square on Rua dos Clerigos is Porto's landmark, the 250-foot Clerigos Tower, offering expansive views over the city and the river.

Continuing south along the Avenida Dom Afonso Henriques, you encounter the cathedral (Se), founded in the 12th century but considerably altered subsequently. It boasts several ornate altars, including an impressive one of silver. Just south of the cathedral is the Guerra Junqueira Museum with an assortment of pottery and tapestries. Across Dom Afonso Henriques is found the Santa Clara Church, elaborately decorated with carved wood. Northeast of here is a well-preserved section of the original town walls.

Hotel Infante de Sagres
Porto

To the west and south of the cathedral area is the town's older quarter. A few blocks in that direction will bring you to the elegant 19th-century Bolsa, or Stock Exchange, with a gigantic neo-Moorish hall. Right behind it is the Sao Francisco Church, decorated in sumptuous baroque and rococo style with carved wood and gilt. East and a bit north of here is the Museum of Ethnography with a regional display illustrating the everyday life of the residents of northern Portugal.

Porto's most important museum is the Museu Soares dos Reis (named for the 19th-century sculptor), housed in an 18th-century palace. It has an extensive collection of Portuguese primitives and sculpture by Soares dos Reis, among other paintings, mostly by Portuguese artists.

The wine to which the city has given its name is mostly produced in the suburb across the river known as VILA NOVA DA GAIA. If you want to see the process and taste the results, take the Dom Luis I Bridge and go to the right as you reach the other side. You will see numerous wineries near the river where the port is fermented in 25,000-gallon vats before being bottled and aged (for 15 years or more). Port officially comes only from the Douro River basin and is fortified with brandy to stop its fermentation, and thus increase the sweetness. Most of these stores may be visited, especially on weekdays during normal business hours.

If you turn left off the bridge instead of right you'll discover the 16th-century convent of Nossa Senhora da Serra do Pilar which has one of the best views of the city climbing up from the banks of the Douro.

If you have the time, an excursion up the coast north of Porto is a worthwhile trip. Take the Rua do Ouro along the river to the west of downtown through SAO JOAO DO FOZ, a suburb sitting right at the mouth of the Douro with a 17th-century fort. Turn north along the Atlantic, past the old Castelo do Queijo, and continue to the new port of LEIXOES, built at the mouth of the Leca River to circumvent problems with silt that plague Porto's channel. A few kilometers after crossing the river to LECA DA PALMEIRA, join N107, passing Porto's Pedras Rubras airport, and turn left on N13.

After a pretty 15 kilometers you will reach VILA DO CONDE, an ancient fishing village which predates the Romans, but which is increasingly attractive as a resort. The town is known for its lace-making and, if you happen to be there on Friday, you will find an especially large selection at the weekly market. The

Santa Clara Convent is worth a visit if only to see the carved ceilings and the tombs of the 14th-century founders, Dom Afonso Sanche and Dona Teresa Martin. In the cloister is a fountain fed by a four-mile-long aqueduct which originates in nearby POVOA DE VARZIM. This neighboring town is also a popular resort due to its nice beach, casino and colorful old fishermen's quarter.

Port to Port

Back to the Beginning

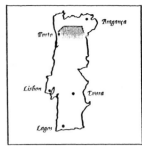

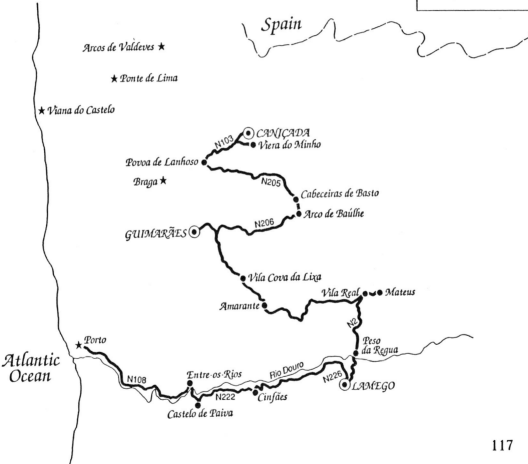

Spain

Arcos de Valdeves ★

★ Ponte de Lima

★ Viana do Castelo

CANIÇADA
N103
Viera do Minho

Povoa de Lanhoso
Braga ★
N205
Cabeceiras de Basto
Arco de Baúlhe
N206
GUIMARÃES

Vila Cova da Lixa
Vila Real ● Mateus
Amarante
N2
Porto
Peso da Regua

Atlantic Ocean
N108
Entre-os-Rios
Rio Douro
N226
N222
Cinfães
LAMEGO
Castelo de Paiva

Back to the Beginning

This is a short itinerary, perfect for a few days' excursion out of Porto into the beautiful, and intensively cultivated, Douro Valley, where the grapes for vinho verde ("green wine") are grown. Because the climate does not allow time for the grapes to ripen fully, the wine produced is relatively light with a slight sparkle. The Douro is a swift river, dropping over 400 feet during its 100-mile journey across Portugal, and carving deep, precipitous canyons into the landscape. The unwieldy geography has not daunted the people who live on the steep but fertile slopes along its banks, however, and the sight of tiny, white villages clinging to the hillsides, surrounded by narrow strips of fields stepping down to the river ranks among the most picturesque in the country. The roads that snake along the top of the cliffs above the river are, as you might expect, small and slow-going, but the views of this magical valley in the heart of Portugal are smashing. The first overnight is in a diminutive inn in the heart of the wine region.

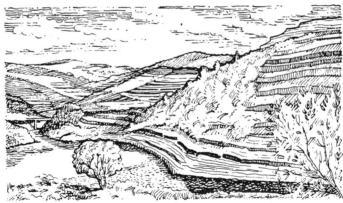

River Douro

The next stop is Guimaraes, a town combining a singular mixture of old and new, where the modern Portuguese nation was born; independence was proclaimed here in the 12th century, and in that sense, it could be considered Portugal's oldest city.   Your hotel, in a stunning converted convent, is, on the other hand, Portugal's newest pousada.

Finally you journey to an impressive natural reserve known as the Peneda-Geres National Park which sits on the country's northern border with Spain and abounds in reservoirs created by damming the numerous rivers which traverse the region. You can survey this magnificent area from on high from the pousada, situated to maximize the beautiful panorama.

ORIGINATING CITY   PORTO
<hr>

Porto is the unofficial capital of northern Portugal and has noteworthy sites to delight the eye and, of course, rich port wine to delight the tastebuds, but the same can be said with assurance about the countryside along the River Douro which winds it way dramatically to the sea through granite slopes covered with vineyards, olive trees and forests.

DESTINATION I   LAMEGO   Estalagem de Lamego
<hr>

Head out of Porto by driving east along the river past tne Maria Pia Bridge until you come to N108.   Turn right and hug the riverbank until just before reaching the town of ENTRE-OS-RIOS, which means "between the rivers," so-named because it stands at the confluence of the Douro and the Tamega.

Cross the Douro in the direction of CASTELO DE PAIVA, a charming little wine town cozily sheltered by intensely green hills. Take N222 east toward CINFAES and, as you pass through the terraced slopes, you'll notice farmers working their fields by hand, just as it has always been done - the steep terrain isn't amenable to modern farm machinery. Most of the houses are on steep hillsides, and appear accessible only on foot. Just before arriving in Cinfaes you pass the Carrapatelo Dam, with what is said to be the largest navigation lock in Europe. Portugal's long-term goal is to make the Douro navigable from Spain to the sea, so the dams have all been built with locks for that eventuality. Besides being the commercial wine center of the vinho verde region, Cinfaes is also known for its handicrafts: weaving, basketry, lace and wood miniatures - a favorite model being the "barco rabelo." These flat-bottomed sailboats were the traditional transporters of goods, especially wine, down the Douro. The shallow drafts were necessary because of the widely varying depth of the water. Today, they have largely been replaced by tanker trucks and the railroad.

Beyond Cinfaes you continue to parallel the river through the neat little town of RESENDE. Another 15 kilometers brings up BARRO, with a good view of the valley. Beyond is SAMODAES and, a bit farther, the MIRADOURO DA BOA VISTA, where you will surely want to stop for some picture-taking. There is a first-rate view of the entire area.

Today's destination, LAMEGO, is just ahead, known as the "museum city" because it retains much of its original Visigothic flavor. To reach the ESTALAGEM DE LAMEGO, a tiny countryside inn, continue through town and take N2 south for a kilometer or so. The estalagem is next to the Raposeira champagne caves, which you should visit while you are here to see the fascinating process by which champagne is made and bottled, and also to sample the result.

Lamego is thought to have been settled first in 500 B.C., and it was later first destroyed then rebuilt by the Romans. It changed hands several times during the Moorish period and was finally retaken definitively in 1037. The first Cortes

Estalagem de Lamego
Lamego

(loosely akin to a parliament) in the young Portuguese nation was held here in 1143 and proclaimed Afonso Henriques as King Afonso I, the first ruler of the Portuguese kingdom (although he had proclaimed himself king in 1139, the act confirmed his status).   In later epochs its importance can be attributed to its situation on the main road connecting Braga and Guimaraes in Portugal to Cordoba and Sevilla in Spain.   Lamego is justly proud of its long history of national importance, and its early reconquest by the Christians is the reason for its surprising number of handsome churches and chapels.

The castle keep looms over town.   The Romanesque structure dates from the 12th century, but the wall around it was built by the Moors in the 11th century to shelter their castle which was on the same spot.   Its underground cistern is unique in Portugal and was probably also a Moorish contribution.

Lamego's cathedral is also 12th-century, but the square tower is all that remains of the original edifice.   The rest was periodically remodelled in the 16th and

17th centuries. The cloisters were added in the 16th century, along with the lovely chapels of Santo Antonio and Sao Nicolau. Across the square and to the right of the cathedral is the former episcopal palace, now housing an attractive museum with early Portuguese paintings, Flemish tapestries, sculpture and antique furniture.

A walk south from the cathedral leads to an area of town with numerous fine, old mansions and palaces of 17th- and 18th-century vintage. At the end of Rua Cardoso Avelino is Lamego's most attractive church, Nossa Senhora do Desterro. It dates from the 17th century and is richly decorated with azulejos and carved wood. Just north of there is the Church of the Holy Cross, also well-appointed within.

On a hill southeast is the beautifully situated Nossa Senhora dos Remedios, an elaborate baroque sanctuary built in the 18th century and dedicated to the patron saint of Lamego. Approximately 700 stairs ascend the hillside, interrupted by landings, pavillions, statues and fountains. If you consider hundreds of steps intimidating, note that the church can also be reached by car from the other side. The view over the town and countryside is spectacular from the terrace of the chapel. This serves as a pilgrimage church during Lamego's annual festival in late August and early September. The festival is one of the country's most famous, and is marked by music of all types, parades and a procession featuring religious figures traditionally drawn by oxen.

Lamego is also noted for its smoked ham and, of course, its white sparkling wine. The city is appealing and typical of the older cities in the interior of Portugal.

Today's drive will take you from one historical city to another even more so, so when you're ready to move on, head north on N2 for a pretty winding journey through vineyards toward PESO DA REGUA, which you bypass. Along the Douro to the east of here is the officially demarcated port wine country. The original royal port wine company was founded here by the Marques de Pombal in 1756 to be sure that the country profited from what was to become a huge industry, originated by Englishmen. One of numerous port-tasting (and purchasing) shops, called Martha's of Armamar, is located just north of Peso da Regua. Signs will be posted but watch for it on your left when you arrive.

Another 25 kilometers and you'll reach VILA REAL, a pleasant town known for its black pottery. From here take N322 east toward MATEUS, picking up N15 toward BRAGANCA. Take the turnoff marked SABROSA and watch for signs indicating "Palacio de Mateus." The beautiful 18th-century Mateus "solar," or manor, set in formal gardens (note the unusual, marble reclining nude in the pool), has tours (guided only) through its spacious rooms, handsomely furnished with antiques from Europe and the former Portuguese Empire (the Orient, Africa, Brazil, etc.), and gorgeous ceilings of carved chestnut. One of the early members of the family was the first governor of Sao Paulo in Brazil. This, of course, is the same family which originated world-famous Mateus Rose wine. If you drink it, you may recognize the mansion from the label.

The actual winery (no longer in the family) is half a kilometer down the road (to the left as you leave the grounds), and is now called SOGRAPE. It is also open to the public at selected hours, and makes an enjoyable stop.

Return to Vila Real and follow the signs toward AMARANTE (and Porto). You can look forward to a scenic, but arduous, 50-kilometer drive on N15, skirting the northern edge of the Serra do Marao and crossing the Tamega River near Amarante. About halfway, you traverse the Alto do Espinho Pass, 3,500 feet up in the Serra. This area was once heavily forested, but fire and an aggressive, if shortsighted, lumber industry have decimated the wooded slopes. Amarante is a pretty country town built up from the Tamega, which is spanned by an 18th-century bridge.

Santa Marinha da Costa
Guimaraes

Follow N15 to the junction with N101 and bear right toward BRAGA. After nine kilometers you reach the typical little village of TROFA, known for its lace making. A picturesque 17 kilometers later you'll arrive in GUIMARAES, known as the "cradle of the Portuguese kingdom" because Afonso Henriques was proclaimed the first king of Portugal here in 1139. Guimaraes also has the singular distinction of being the only town in the country with two pousadas. Both are charming but, due to its utterly unique ambiance, we recommend the newest member of the chain, the SANTA MARINHA DA COSTA, which sits magnificently above town on the site of a 12th-century convent. The convent was founded in 1154 by the wife of Afonso Henriques, but evidence uncovered during the construction of the pousada suggests that there was a much earlier structure here - perhaps dating back as far as the 8th century. In the 17th century the convent was turned over to the Hieronymites and almost totally rebuilt in a later style.

As befits the first capital of the nation, Guimaraes retains one of the best-preserved castles in the country, constructed in the 10th century, but extensively restored in the 1930s. Afonso Henriques was born here in 1110, so the castle has a symbolic significance for the nation. There are fine views from the narrow, multi-towered ramparts.

At the foot of the hill is the 15th-century Paco dos Duques, built by the first Duke of Braganca, a member of the powerful Portuguese family which furnished the country with its monarchs after 1640. The seat of the Ducal family was transferred to Vila Vicosa at a later point and the palace was abandoned. It has since been restored (in the 20th century), and merits a visit for its superior antiques - paintings, furniture, tapestries, porcelain, weapons, etc. - and striking chestnut ceilings.

In the old quarter of town around the Largo da Oliveira (and the other pousada), is a network of ancient, picturesque streets and squares reflecting the town's medieval past. Also there is the church of Nossa Senhora da Oliveira, founded in the 12th century by Afonso Henriques. It was since expanded, and the Manueline tower was added in the 16th century. The adjoining building of the former Dominican monastery now houses the Alberto Sampaio Museum with an interesting collection of Portuguese art.

Time permitting, a memorable excursion is to the nearby mountain peak of PENHA. Take N101 toward Amarante and turn left just past MESAO FRIO, for the 20-kilometer round trip. The views from the top are outstanding.

The next destination features spectacular scenery in the Peneda-Geres National Park.   Leave Guimaraes on N101 toward Amarante, then bear left on N206 toward FAFE.   If you're paying attention to the map you'll notice that this is not the most direct route to your destination, but it takes you through some unforgettable country.   SAO ROMAO DE AROES has an early 13th-century Romanesque church, and the picturesque little village of Fafe has some handsome 18th- and 19th-century mansions built by families who returned after making their fortunes in colonial Brazil.   Another 28 kilometers through beautiful landscape brings ARCO DE BAULHO into view, where you turn left on N205, coming next to the ancient settlement of CABECEIRAS DE BASTO, with a large monastery built mostly in the 18th century (though founded much earlier).   You'll come shortly to the Nossa Senhora do Porto Reservoir on the Ave River, after which you pass through several quaint villages before reaching POVOA DE LANHOSO where there is a ruined 12th-century castle with stellar views from its hilltop perch.

Take N103 east to begin your approach to the park through wooded hills.   After about 20 kilometers watch for the sign directing you left toward today's destination, the POUSADA DE SAO BENTO, a cozy lodge majestically situated on the edge of the nature park and overlooking the giant blue Canicada Reservoir far below, set like an aquamarine in the valley.

If hiking in untamed forest brimming with wildlife piques your interest, plan to spend some time here.   Almost every conceivable outdoor recreation is a possibility here: horseback riding (and horse-drawn carriage rides, for the less hearty), aquatic sports on the reservoirs, mountain climbing, etc.   Guided tours of the park are available, and enchanting, or in one day you can easily make the drive from the pousada to the little spa of GERES and on to PORTELA DO

HOMEM on the Spanish border, with plenty of time for stops along the way. The old Roman road from Braga to Spain passed this way, and you can still see some of the ancient milestones which marked the route.

This is an ideal spot for relaxation, free of the seduction of sights other than peaceful forest and cool, blue mountain lakes.

Pousada de Sao Bento
Vieira do Minho

Back to the Beginning

Romantic River Routes

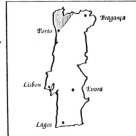

129

Romantic River Routes

This itinerary takes you through the extreme northwest corner of Portugal, the area known as the "Verde Minho," referring to the green Minho River region. And it is an apt description; its intensely cultivated fields and its heavily forested mountain slopes envelop the visitor in green.

Culturally, the area shares a great deal with its Spanish neighbor to the north, Galicia. The Galician language and the dialect of northern Portugal resemble each other, and the similarity of other characteristics - architecture, folk dances, music, traditional dress, food, wine - is striking. This is the most densely populated section of the country and also the coolest and the rainiest. The economy is primarily agricultural - the majority of the small family farms are still cultivated and harvested much the same as they have been for generations.

Dolmen

The Verde Minho also encompasses what is technically the oldest part of Portugal: the part that was declared a separate kingdom by Afonso Henriques in 1139. A result is that there are a large number of Romanesque monuments. There are also lots of churches, attesting to the Minhotos' reputation as extremely pious people who are renowned for their gay religious festivals and popular pilgrimages. It's one of the last areas where you may see local citizens in traditional dress even when it's not festival time.

Local handicrafts run the gamut from lace to knife blades, with no particular one being especially predominant. The town markets, therefore, offer a wide variety of interesting possibilities for your shopping pleasure. A typical and hearty regional dish is "caldo verde," a creamy cabbage and potato soup. "Bacalhau," or dried cod, is perhaps even more ubiquitous here than in the rest of the country.

ORIGINATING CITY   PORTO

Porto occupies a privileged location at the mouth of the River Douro, and serves as the economic hub of northern Portugal. But the area north of the city to the Spanish border presents some very attractive contrasts to the cosmopolitan air of the country's second-largest city. It is a region sprinkled with quaint villages set in the verdant landscape of vineyards and fertile river valleys (the Ave, the Cavado, the Lima, and, of course, the Minho), an intriguing mixture of an ancient society and young wine.

Leave Porto heading north through the suburbs on N13 and bear right on N14 toward BRAGA, bypassing the largely industrial VILA NOVA DE FAMALICAO, where you pick up N204 going northwest.   Just beyond the village of GAMIL, turn left on N103 to BARCELOS, center of a thriving handicraft region.   You cross the Cavado River on an interesting 15th-century bridge as you enter town. If you happen to be here on Thursday, you will see everything from pottery to basketry to linen displayed at the open market in the huge main square called the "Campo da Republica" in the center of town.   On any other day you should visit the Centro de Artesanato in the Largo da Porta Nova, just off the southwest corner of the square, which sells a wide variety of local handicrafts.   It is housed in a tower remaining from the 16th-century town fortifications.   Nearby is the 18th-century municipal garden with pretty baroque fountains and ornate walls.

By far the most famous folk-art ceramic around here (and perhaps in all of Portugal) is the "Galo de Barcelos," or Barcelos cock, a multicolored rooster, available in all sizes which you'll find for sale throughout the country.   The cock symbolizes this ancient legend: A Galician was passing through Barcelos on his way to Santiago de Compostela in Spain.   He was accused and convicted of a crime and, during his final plea at the judge's house, he exclaimed in frustration, "As certainly as I am innocent, it is equally certain that that cock will rise up and crow when I am hanged."   The chicken in question was a roasted one on the judge's dinner table and the pilgrim's claim provoked much laughter among those present.   He was taken off to be hanged and, of course, at the proper moment the roasted chicken arose and crowed.   The judge managed to get to the gallows before the poor fellow died and had him released.   He returned to Barcelos many years later and built a monument to St. James, which is now in the Archaeological Museum of the city.

Hotel do Elevador
Braga

The Archaeological Museum, partially open-air, is housed in the former palace of the Dukes of Braganca, as is the Regional Ceramics Museum, a collection of colorful native pottery. The palace is located a few blocks southwest of the main square, near the bridge across the Cavado, where you can also see the parish church with its fine azulejos. Opposite the palace is the Solar dos Pinheiros, a 15th-century granite mansion which is representative of other admirable old mansions in the vicinity.

When you are ready to continue, return on N103 across the Cavado and remain on it to BRAGA, your destination for today. This is one of the country's oldest cities, and was once the seat of the Portuguese monarchy. To reach your hotel, continue through town to the east, following the signs for CHAVES, then bear right toward BOM JESUS DO MONTE. The shady, switchback road winds up to a plateau on top of the hill, where you'll find the HOTEL DO ELEVADOR, built into the hillside 700 feet above the city with a spectacular view over the valley below.

The church of Bom Jesus do Monte was built in late neoclassical style by a local architect, Carlos Amarante, in the late 18th century. It was designed as a pilgrimage church, and the vast 900-meter stairway (leading from the base of the hill to its summit) represents the stations of the cross with chapels at each landing. One segment is called the Stairway of the Five Senses, and another the Stairway of the Virtues, with the senses and virtues represented by tiled fountains. You might want to take the stairs down, then return by the "elevador" (funicular) back up. Inquire about timetables at the hotel desk.

Braga was probably settled by the Celts long before the Romans arrived in 250 B.C. It was an important Roman town, subsequently occupied by the Suevi, the Goths and the Moors before being reconquered by the Christians in the 11th century. It became the center of the religious hierarchy in the area and maintained that status until the 18th century. This presence resulted in the great number of architectural monuments which now dot the town.

A very attractive city, Braga is now Portugal's fourth largest (after Lisbon, Porto and Coimbra) and is developing some industrial installations. It has the inevitable urban development at the edge of town, but the older central area retains a great deal of its traditional charm and ambiance.

The old town is dominated by the cathedral. Originally built in the 11th century, only the south doorway (Porta do Sol), the apse of the cloister and some minor trim remain from that period. Other elements, including the numerous small chapels, were later additions, and the interior was redone in 18th-century baroque. The Anca-stone high altar is especially interesting. Reached from the courtyard, the Gothic Capela dos Reis contains the tombs of Henry of Burgundy and his wife - parents of the first king, Afonso Henriques - along with the mummified body of a former archbishop.

Across the street to the north is the former archbishop's palace which has three separate wings dating from the 14th, 17th and 18th centuries. One wing now houses one of the country's most important libraries. East of there is the Torre de Menagem (keep) which survives from the town's 14th-century fortifications. Behind the tower are formal gardens. To the south is the 16th-century Capela dos Coimbras whose interior is prettily decorated with azulejos and sculpture. If you continue east to the Avenida da Liberdade and turn right, then right again on Rua do Raio, you'll find the Fonte do Idolo, said to be of pre-Roman origin. At the end of that street is the Palacio do Raio (or do Mexicano) which typifies the numerous 18th-century mansions in Braga.

Braga is designed for wandering and savoring the old-world atmosphere of its colorful, landscaped squares and charming, narrow cobblestoned streets. If you find yourself in town at mealtime, try the Restaurante Inacio at the west end of town near the Campo das Hortas, a restaurant with good, and inexpensive, regional food. The flaming souffle is a spectacular dessert (and lighter than it looks, lest you think you don't have room).

A fascinating excursion from Braga is to the pre-Roman ruins at CITANIA DE BRITEIROS. The settlement, apparently of Celtic origin (3rd century B.C.), is about 10 kilometers southwest of town (watch for signs as you descend Bom Jesus do Monte). Drive through the gate up to the caretaker's house to buy your ticket. The ruins of three defensive walls encircle the village, consisting of some 150 large and small structures. Of particular interst are the circular houses. There are remains of fountains, aqueducts and a funeral monument in the 10-acre site, the most impressive and largest in Portugal. The site also has a wonderful view over the surrounding valleys.

Today's journey ventures more deeply into the Minho countryside.   Take N201 northwest from Braga toward PONTE DE LIMA, passing through SAO JERONIMO DO REAL.   Just out of town to the northwest is the Chapel of Sao Frutuoso dos Montelios, one of Portugal's oldest Christian monuments. Although still the subject of controversy, it was apparently built in the 7th century, partially destroyed by the Moors, and rebuilt in the 11th century; thus a mixture of Byzantine (uncommon in Portugal) and Gothic influences.   It seems to have originally had the form of a Greek cross, but parts of it were destroyed in the building of the adjacent Church of Sao Francisco, an 18th-century monastery church.

Return to N201 and continue north.   You traverse intense-green, wooded hills with vineyards for the next 27 kilometers until you reach Ponte de Lima, which means "Bridge over the Lima River".   The ancient, Roman stone bridge has 15 large arches and 12 small ones.   The town is delightfully situated on the bank of the Lima amid lush, rolling hills, and has a wonderful old-world ambiance.   It has been settled since Roman times, as the bridge suggests, and traces of its medieval fortifications are interspersed among the more modern white houses near the end of the bridge.   If you can arrange to be here on Monday, you will enjoy the famous market on the river bank, which has taken place for several centuries.   Numerous shops also display the varied handicrafts of the region, including blankets and baskets.   The tourist office has a modest exhibit of regional handicrafts.

When you're ready to move on, take N202 north in the direction of the village of REFOIOS.   After about four kilometers look for a sign indicating a left turn for CALHEIROS and BRANDARA, which, after another kilometer, will bring you to the PACO DE CALHEIROS, your hotel for tonight, which you will have caught glimpses of at several points on the way up. This stop is not really in a town, but is an elegant, private mansion set in the green countryside and surrounded by vineyards. Drive through the stone gates on your right and enter the 14th century.

Paco de Calheiros
Calheiros

DESTINATION III   VALENCA DO MINHO   Pda. de Sao Teotonio

If you can tear yourself away from Calheiros, you can continue through the beautiful Minho area to its northern extreme - the river itself and the border with the Spanish region of Galicia. Return to N202, and turn left past Refoios to SOUTO, where you bear right toward PONTE DA BARCA, another picturesque little country town on the Lima River. Head north from there on N101, being sure to look back toward town after crossing the 16th-century bridge for a splendid view. A few kilometers farther and you reach the lovely village of ARCOS DE VALDEVEZ, straddling the Vez River.

As you continue north toward the border you are treated to glorious landscapes and quaint little villages. After about 17 kilometers watch for a panoramic viewpoint toward the Serra de Peneda to the east and the Lima Valley to the south. Twelve kilometers later you pass the large, 19th-century Palacio da Brejoeira on your left. Soon thereafter you reach the border town of MONCAO, on the bank of the Minho. Being on the border with Spain, Moncao has a long history of heroic defense of the Portuguese frontier, and the ruins of the 14th-century castle attest to its age-old territorial prerogative. The parish church is Romanesque, begun in the 13th century, and has a pretty interior. The town is also famous as a source of vinho verde, the youthful regional wine.

Pousada de Sao Teotonio
Valenca do Minho

Remain on N101, which now continues westward, paralleling the mighty Minho River. After five kilometers you pass LAPELA, a tiny town clustered around its ancient defensive tower. Continue through the intensively farmed river bank with endless vineyards and cultivated terraces to your destination, VALENCA DO MINHO, a popular border-crossing town which faces the Spanish town of Tuy on the right bank. As you follow the signs to your hotel, the POUSADA DE SAO TEOTONIO, enter the fortified old city which sits on a hill above the newer, lower town. The pousada is located on a point of the ancient fort and commands a breathtaking view of the river, the Eiffel-designed International Bridge, the town of Tuy and the Galician mountains beyond.

The northern fortified section was begun in the 13th century by Dom Sancho I, and traces its origin to Roman times. The section to the south was added in the 17th century, after the Spanish monarchy had relinquished control over Portugal. This area is popularly called the "Coroada" because of the crown-like shape of its layout, and is joined to the older part by a stone bridge. The stronghold consists of double curtain walls, numerous bastions and watch towers, all of which offer lovely vistas over the surrounding region.

The well-preserved fortress retains a wonderful medieval atmosphere which will reward you for the time dedicated to strolling and shopping in the many souvenir shops along the narrow, winding, cobblestone streets. The ancient stone houses and fountains recapture the enchantment of a time long past.

A short excursion from here is to nearby (seven kilometers) MONTE DE FARO on N101-1. Ascend through forested slopes to a parking area, then walk up to the top for unforgettable views.

DESTINATION IV   VIANA DO CASTELO   Hotel de Santa Luzia

Today we follow the Minho to where it pours into the Atlantic, then continue to the mouth of the Lima River and the lovely city which serves as the capital of the Minho region. Leave Valenca southward on N13, which generally parallels the broad, beautiful Minho to its end. The river gradually widens as it nears the sea. After 15 kilometers you come to VILA NOVA DA CERVEIRA, a typical little town perched over the river. One of Portugal's most interesting pousadas is here (see the hotel listings) and would make a good place for lunch if you got a late start. The inn occupies an entire fort with the rooms located in reconstructed old houses. The streets inside the pousada constitute a tiny village, including a beautiful 18th-century chapel, with the restaurant rising from the castle ramparts and overlooking the river. The original fort was constructed by Dom Dinis in the 14th century, but much of it was added later. It was inhabited as late as 1975. You'll find the pousada in the plaza just a couple of blocks off the highway. There is also a nice handicrafts shop next door with local ceramics, lace and needlework.

Continue south on scenic N13 along the Minho through several small villages to the ancient town of CAMINHA, once a defensive bastion opposing Monte Santa Tecla across the river in Spain. Today a simple fishing village, it has retained a lovely medieval atmosphere apparent in the main square with its old clock tower. The 15th- to 16th-century parish church, found on the street leading from the arch under the tower, has a particularly fine carved ceiling.

Still heading south on N13, you skirt the beaches of the Atlantic and pass a number of quaint seaside towns, some wonderful old beach homes, and a few modern beach developments. In VILA PRAIA DA ANCORA there is an extremely well-preserved dolmen, a solitary testament to settlement here as long as 4000 years ago. To find it, take the turn to the left for Ponte de Lima to the sign V. P. ANCORA, then take another left. About 100 feet toward town look for a small, hard-to-see plaque in a stone wall saying MONUMENTO DOLMEN DA BAIRROSA and enter the courtyard behind the wall.

Back on N13, another 15 kilometers brings you to VIANA DO CASTELO, the largest city in the Minho, north of Braga, and your destination for tonight. Follow the signs for MONTE SANTA LUZIA, a hill north of town, to reach the classic HOTEL DE SANTA LUZIA, perched serenely on the mountain, commanding spectacular views of the city and the river where it meets the sea.

Hotel de Santa Luzia
Viana do Castelo

Although apparently of Greek origin, Viana do Castelo became a boom town in the 16th century when Portuguese sailing skills paved the way for fishing the Newfoundland cod area. That period of prosperity is reflected in one of the town's most attractive features: the fine old mansions in the central section near the Praca da Republica. There is also a nice 16th-century fountain in the square and several handsome public buildings. A bit south of the square is the 14th-century parish church which contains some fine wood carving. Take the time to absorb the mood.

A few blocks west of the square is the Municipal Museum with a worthwhile collection of antique furniture from the once-far-flung Portuguese Empire, and colorful azulejos on the interior walls. At the west end of town near the river is a 16th-century fort built by Phillip II of Spain during his reign on the Portuguese throne.

If the timing of your trip is flexible, try to be here around the middle of August when Viana is the site of one of the country's most famous religious pilgrimages. The celebration is characterized by folk dancing, fireworks and parades.

PORTUGAL

Map of Portugal with Hotel Locations

Once home to the Count of Santa Eulalia family, this 17th-century grand manor house is now owned by the Honorable Colin Clark, a documentary film-maker who divides his time between Portugal, England and the United States.   The small stone palace (paco), with its book-end towers, is isolated on a hillside surrounded by garden and vineyards.   A sixty-foot arched and shaded verandah overlooks the rich green valley and an unusual stone swimming pool with a fountain in the center.   Inside, careful restoration creates a feeling of having stepped back 300 years in time.   The grand, long beautifully tiled main entry hall has twenty-foot stone ceilings.   Off the hall and downstairs you discover a library, music room, game room, dining room with one large table and a cozy sitting area with open fireplace - all accented with handsome antiques.   The three guestrooms in the main house - blue, yellow and the master - are spacious, opulent and have cavernous marble bathrooms.   Across the garden, the former stables have been converted into seven additional rooms, necessarily more modern, smaller, less interesting and about $20 less expensive.   The paco is off N202 between Ponte de Lima and Arcos.   Watch for the road to Jolda, and follow it to a fork pointing to Sao Lourenco.   Turn right and see a sign on the left to Paco da Gloria.

PACO DA GLORIA
Jolda Madalena
4970 Arcos de Valdevez, Portugal
tel: 58-941477
10 rooms - Moderate
Closed: November to March
Credit cards: VS
Private manor house, Pool
Nearest airport: Porto (90 km)
Nearest train station: Viana do Castelo (30 km)

The Paloma Blanca (White Dove), originally a beautiful private home built in the early 1930s, was in the process of more than doubling its size when we visited Aveiro. The manager proudly showed us the new construction, while explaining the painstaking measures being taken to remain faithful to the original structure. By summer of 1987 the new and the old should be a harmonious whole of pale yellow stucco with red tile roof and wooden balconies - all surrounded by garden which should soon feature a swimming pool. Inside, the hotel is unpretentious and comfortable. The high-ceilinged, smallish bedrooms are found off rambling hallways. They are simply decorated with attractive, regional-style wood furniture, and pretty woven throw-rugs that pick up the earthtones in the cloth-like wallpaper. The bathrooms are small and modern. All the rooms have televisions - an unusual feature in Portugal. There are a few larger rooms (for four people) which, if available, will be let as doubles. It is worth requesting a room away from the noise of Aveiro's streets. There are plans to build a restaurant, but when we were there only breakfast was served in a cozy and charming second-floor room overlooking the garden. The handsome ceilings here and in the tiny bar on the ground floor are original and lovingly preserved. The Paloma Blanca offers an intimate atmosphere for a city hotel.

PALOMA BLANCA
Rua Luis Gomes de Carvalho, 23
3800 Aveiro, Portugal
tel: 34-26039   telex: 37353
22 rooms - Budget
Credit cards: none
Friendly staff, Pool
Nearest airport: Porto (70 km)
Nearest train station: Aveiro

On N10, just outside of Azeitao (home of Lancers wine), is the enchanting and peaceful Quinta das Torres inn, surrounded by thirty-four acres of farmland. Sculpted gardens and a large stone pond complete with pavillion and swan add to the idyllic scene.   A private manor house for centuries, Quinta das Torres was built in 1580 as a palace for the Count of Aveiro.   The family of the proprietors have called this home for over a hundred years, offering guests accommodation since 1931.   The ivy-covered, low stone structure surrounds a central patio with fountain.   The main house contains splendid, if not perfectly preserved, public rooms, a good restaurant, the private rooms of the residing family members and a tiny chapel where mass is said on Sundays.   A suite occupies a corner of the main house, and comprises an enormous sitting room with fireplace, a large colorfully tiled bedroom with brass, white-canopied beds and a stone terrace overlooking the orange groves which provide fresh juice for breakfast - and all for just a few additional dollars.   Across the patio are the remaining bedrooms, each different in size and decoration, and all furnished with antiques; electric blankets and modern plumbing being among the few concessions to progress.   A sampling: #6, our favorite, has a fireplace and canopy beds; #10 has wonderful trundle-type beds and a huge bath; and #2 has a private balcony.

QUINTA DAS TORRES
Estrada Nacional
2925 Azeitao, Portugal
tel: 20-80001
12 rooms - Budget
Credit cards: none
Restaurant, Extensive grounds
Nearest airport: Lisbon (23 km)
Nearest train station: Setubal (12 km)

One of the most recent entries into the pousada network, this inn was built in 1972.   Though notably lacking in historical ambiance, it offers every modern convenience as well as an excellent central location.   The pousada is just off the main Lisbon-Porto highway, and just opposite one of Portugal's premium sightseeing attractions: the 15th-century Batalha monastery, after whose architect it is named.   The pousada is well-appointed and pleasant, with comfortable, mostly modern wood furnishings throughout.   The bedrooms are of average size, with high ceilings and relatively spacious bathrooms.   The decor in the bedrooms has a distinctly, though perhaps accidentally, American western flavor; one repeated in the cowhide rugs in the hallways and the wood ceilings and leather furniture in the lounge.   The restaurant is quite good - the beef fondue merits special praise - and overlooks the famous monastery; it features an outdoor terrace which is enjoyable in fine weather.   Though likely to be remembered more for its convenience than its atmosphere, the Mestre Afonso Domingues provides an ideal base for numerous sightseeing excursions, or the perfect overnight stop before or after visiting Batalha monastery.

POUSADA DO MESTRE AFONSO DOMINGUES
2440 Batalha, Portugal
tel: 44-96260 telex: 42339
20 rooms - Moderate
Credit cards: all major
Restaurant, Excellent location
U.S. Rep: Marketing Ahead
Rep. tel: (212) 686-9213
Nearest airport: Lisbon (112 km)
Nearest train station: Pombal (53 km)

Historic Braga is a must-see city.   Although, on its own merit the Hotel do Elevador would not normally be included, in our opinion it is the best choice for accommodation in the vicinity of Braga.   Just a few kilometers from Braga, atop the Bom Jesus do Monte - a major sight in its own right - you find the Hotel do Elevador named for its proximity to the funicular which transports sightseers up and down the mountain.   Around 100 years old, the two-story hotel is built down the mountainside facing Braga.   Renovated in 1967, it provides contemporary, if a tad dowdy, comfort to travellers who want a touring base in this area.   Apart from the reception (very friendly) and a few bedrooms, the main level is devoted to a lounge/bar with comfortable, well-worn furniture and the glassed-in restaurant which juts out over the hillside and the sculpted rear garden.   The food is only adequate, but the view is outstanding.   The majority of the bedrooms are downstairs - all have panoramic views of the city below. Bedrooms come in two sizes: spacious and twice as spacious (for a well-spent $8 more).   The larger rooms have a foyer entrance, bigger bathroom, and an extra table and chairs.   The decor is a curious blend of comfy armchairs, oriental rugs, pseudo-antique beds and colorfully flowered drapes at wood-framed windows - an eclectic mixture that provides a pleasant ambiance.

HOTEL DO ELEVADOR
Bom Jesus do Monte
4700 Braga, Portugal
tel: 53-25011
25 rooms - Inexpensive
Credit cards: all major
Restaurant, Good views, Quiet
Nearest airport: Porto (60 km)
Nearest train station: Braga (6 km)

This hotel is aptly named, as it is housed within an ornate, 19th-century royal palace - owned by the government since the Portuguese republic was formed. Before its politically expedient exit in the early 20th century, the royal family enjoyed luxury, tranquility and hunting in this retreat, encircled by elegant gardens and thick pine forest.   The hotel is private; the space is leased from the government which, incidentally, supplies the magnificent antiques you discover in the public rooms, each of which resembles a museum exhibit, creating the impression of a collector gone crazy.   The bedrooms have 15-foot ceilings, and each is handsomely furnished, with many original pieces.   Many bedrooms overlook the lovely sculpted gardens, laden with flowers in the spring and summer.   Double rooms vary in size, however, so you should request a large room when you make a reservation, which is recommended as this is a justifiably popular stop.   The restaurant is the piece de resistance, with elaborately carved arched windows, gleaming multi-hued wood parquet floor, and a three-dimensional painted wood ceiling which sparkles with pinpoints of light.   To this beautiful setting add fine food, an extensive wine list and attentive service.   At the Palace Hotel do Bucaco, an enchanting location, opulent atmosphere and fine food combine to provide you with an unforgettable stay.

PALACE HOTEL DO BUCACO
Bucaco
3050 Mealhada, Portugal
tel: 31-93101 telex: 53049
60 rooms - Expensive
Credit cards: all major
Restaurant, Beautiful setting
Nearest airport: Porto (110 km)
Nearest train station: Luso (4 km)

Just a few kilometers northeast of the lively and lovely seaside town of Aveiro, this square, red roadside inn is an interesting melange of modern comfort and pseudo-antique-style decor. Lots of wood and leather accent the lounge, bar and the attractive blue-and-white restaurant, which offers above-average fare and excels at enormous seafood specialty dishes. The bedrooms are upstairs off long hallways with arched, brick ceilings. All are carpeted with an unusual royal blue carpet patterned with gold escutcheons. The antique-reproduction furnishings are quite handsome, particularly in the doubles and suites, whose dark-wood "bilros" beds are more elaborately carved and ornate than those in the twins. All the bedrooms have high, white, wood-plank ceilings, white bedspreads and tiled bathrooms. Curiously, bright flowered wallpaper provides a colorfully disharmonious note to the otherwise appealing bedrooms. The suites, for an additional $5, are extremely spacious and feature a larger bathroom, and small sitting rooms with television. The Albergaria's location, on the main road into Aveiro, makes it very convenient and easy to find. But, this also means that the front rooms are noisy, so request a room overlooking the fields at the back of the hotel. The friendly staff will strive to make your stay pleasant in every way.

ALBERGARIA DE JOAO PADEIRO
Cacia
3800 Aveiro, Portugal
tel: 34-91326
27 rooms - Budget
Credit cards: all major
Restaurant, Convenient location
Nearest airport: Porto (55 km)
Nearest train station: Aveiro (6 km)

The most outstanding representative of the noble homes in the region, the Calheiros palace is situated seven kilometers from Ponte de Lima on the road to Arcos de Valdevez (N202).   Watch for a sign to Calheiros and Brandara.   You will see the imposing stone and plaster palace encircled by grape vines as you ascend approximately two kilometers to its grand stone gates.   The property has been in Count Francisco Lopes de Calheiros family since 1336 when it was granted to them by King Dom Dinis in 1336.   This stunning property is exquisitely restored and maintained.   A fountain plays in front, and elegant sculpted gardens grace the back lawn, which offers a commanding view of the surrounding countryside.   Each of the bedrooms is a gem, having thick stone walls (some with windowseats), and all are simply appointed with obviously genuine, family antiques.   The dark wood beds are exceptionally lovely, no two alike, and all topped with sparkling white spreads.   All have gleaming modern bathrooms. Family heirlooms abound throughout the striking public rooms, many of which have elaborate fireplaces - one a walk-in stone hearth.   The severely handsome dining room usually serves only breakfast.

PACO DE CALHEIROS
Calheiros
4990 Ponte de Lima, Portugal
tel: 58-941364
8 rooms - Moderate
Credit cards: none
Private manor house
Nearest airport: Porto (98 km)
Nearest train station: Viana do Castelo (28 km)

Near the train station and just a half-hour from Lisbon, the Albatroz is a delightful discovery, combining the charm of a country inn with the luxury of a five-star hotel.   A villa built for King Dom Manuel II in the 19th century, it has been enlarged and renovated to provide its guests with quiet, understated elegance amid the bustle of old Cascais.   The hotel hugs a rocky outcropping on the beautiful coastline of the Bay of Cascais, twenty-five of the forty bedrooms command spectacular views.   In the original villa there are eleven bedrooms, a commodious bar and the restaurant.   The Albatroz restaurant is elegantly decorated in pale beige and white, has a marble and wood floor and is well-known for its seafood.   The eleven bedrooms in the original villa have a charming old-world flavor, with high, sculpted ceilings and stone windows - no two are alike in size or decor.   The balance of the bedrooms are in the newer part, as is the beautiful lounge which looks across the broad stone patio with its turquoise swimming pool to the bay.   These newer bedrooms are spacious and tastefully appointed, though more contemporary in style, decorated in soft colors and furnished in warm wood.   The bayside rooms also have terraces.

HOTEL ALBATROZ
Rua Frederico Arouca, 100
2750 Cascais, Portugal
tel: 1-282821 telex: 16052
40 rooms - Very expensive
Credit cards: all major
Restaurant, Sea views, Pool
U.S. Rep: Marketing Ahead
Rep. tel: (212) 686-9213
Nearest airport: Lisbon (35 km)
Nearest train station: Cascais

On the seaside road between Cascais and the Praia do Guincho is a captivating inn recently opened by Bernardo Monteiro (a hotelier) and his brother and sister (both economists).   In 1983, the family acquired the fifty-year-old property and within a year reopened its doors to offer guests very special accommodation combined with personalized service.   The inn has enjoyed such popularity that a ten-room annex was opened in spring, 1986.   The focal point of the main house is its welcoming lounge with its polished hardwood floor, oriental rugs, marble fireplace and cozy antiques.   It has a gleaming wood bar at one end and sliding glass doors lead out to a shady verandah overlooking the pool and the sparkling sea.   Breakfast can be taken on the verandah, in your room or at the poolside restaurant.   There is also an intimate dining room downstairs.   A spectacular crystal and wood stairway leads upstairs to the high-ceilinged, whitewashed bedrooms - comfortably old-fashioned, well-proportioned and decorated in deep green and beige.   Bedrooms with lovely sea views command a higher price as do the spacious suites.   The annex rooms all overlook the sea from either porch or balcony, but they are smaller and more austere - furnished in pale wood and decorated in pastel peach and stark white.

ESTALAGEM SENHORA DA GUIA
Estrada do Guincho, Cascais, Portugal
tel: 1-289239 telex: 42111
28 rooms - Expensive
Credit cards: all major
Restaurant, Sea views, Pool
U.S. Rep: Marketing Ahead
Rep. tel: (212) 686-9213
Nearest airport: Lisbon (40 km)
Nearest train station: Cascais (2 km)

Originally built as an inn, the Santa Luzia, in the picturesque Roman town of Elvas, has been a pousada since the 1940s. The inn's major claim to fame is its kitchen, which prepares delectable regional specialties such as "bacalhau a braz", "carne de porco a alentejana" and the wonderfully sweet dessert "siricaia", all served in abundance and with a smile. Be sure to go with a big appetite. As it is just a dozen kilometers from the border, neighboring Spaniards have discovered the large, bustling restaurant and, on Sundays in particular, you are likely to hear more Spanish than Portuguese. Though quite pleasant in a comfortable worn way, the pousada is in need of a general facelift and, recognizing this, plans are going ahead to remodel throughout and add twenty bedrooms. Currently, the bedrooms are on the small side, with high, whitewashed ceilings and simple, regional wood furnishings. When the crowds of diners disperse, a cozy atmosphere prevails in the bar and the lounge with their dark wood and leather furniture. In addition, the staff is among the most gracious we encountered in Portugal.

POUSADA DE SANTA LUZIA
Estrada Nacional
7350 Elvas, Portugal
tel: 68-62194 telex: 12469
11 rooms - Moderate
Credit cards: all major
Excellent restaurant
U.S. Rep: Marketing Ahead
Rep. tel: (212) 686-9213
Nearest airport: Lisbon (222 km)
Nearest train station: Elvas (3 km)

In 1259, King Dom Afonso III, recognizing the strategic importance of the town, commissioned a castle to be built in Estremoz.   In 1497 Dom Manuel met a gentleman named Vasco de Gama here and entrusted him with the command of the armada that took him to India.   In 1698, a fire destroyed all but the Tower of the Three Crowns (so-called because its construction was carried out under the reign of three kings), and Joao V had an armory built over the ruins.   From the mid-19th to mid-20th century, it was a military barracks, then briefly a School of Industry and Commerce before being converted into one of Portugal's most elegant pousadas in 1969.   Thanks to careful restoration and decoration, using scores of 17th- and 18th-century antiques, the castle today appears much as it must have under Joao V.   A grand marble staircase leads upstairs to high, wide hallways lined with beautiful antiques and an impressive collection of "contador" chests.   The bedrooms are regal; each one unique, but all spacious, decorated in rich colors and sumptuously furnished with antiques and handsome reproductions.   Views are either of the countryside and town, or over the interior garden courtyard.   The restaurant, with its massive stone pillars and arched ceiling, offers excellent fare in a romantic setting.

POUSADA RAINHA SANTA ISABEL
Castelo de Estremoz, 7100 Estremoz, Portugal
tel: 68-22618 telex: 43885
23 rooms - Expensive
Credit cards: all major
Restaurant, Medieval building
U.S. Rep: Marketing Ahead
Rep. tel: (212) 686-9213
Nearest airport: Lisbon (190 km)
Nearest train station: Estremoz

A captivating city, Evora rises clean and white from the Alentejo plains. Within its walls is a superior pousada, originally a 15th-century private mansion built on the ruins of the old Evora castle.   Over the course of the centuries it has been enlarged and embellished, serving as a monastery for the Loios monks, whose chapel (now privately owned) flanks it still.   The government rescued it from ruin by restoring it to its former glory and converting it into an elegant inn. Cathedral ceilings are supported by cool granite and marble arches around which are nestled the cozy sofas and chairs of the spacious lounge.   An ornately carved, wide marble staircase leads upstairs to broad hallways and diminutive red-tiled bedrooms (the original monastic cells), charmingly appointed with hand-carved chestnut armoirs and beds topped with crisp linen and white bedspreads.   There is an extraordinary sitting room upstairs, intricately hand-painted from floor to ceiling and furnished with beautiful antiques.   The glassed-in dining room, though serving only average fare, is nonetheless worth visiting for its unique ambiance.   Arranged around the interior garden cloister and whispering fountain, its tables are tucked amidst slender, carved pillars.

POUSADA DOS LOIOS
Largo Conde de Vila Flor
7000 Evora, Portugal
tel: 69-24051 telex: 43288
32 rooms - Expensive
Restaurant, 15th-century castle
Credit cards: all major
U.S. Rep: Marketing Ahead
Rep. tel: (212) 686-9213
Nearest airport: Lisbon (145 km)
Nearest train station: Evora

Over 100 years ago, a Portuguese sardine magnate constructed an elegant family townhome on a quiet square in the peaceful fishing village of Faro. Today that house is a small pension on a busy square in the capital city of the Algarve, owned and run by an English family. The square, two-story granite and whitewashed building fronts the square directly and has iron grilles and balconies. The main floor contains two bedrooms, an attractive and good dining room and a small bar. In the summertime, a popular outdoor bar is set up under the grape arbors in the courtyard. From here, stairs lead up to a small, brick, rooftop terrace, used for sunning during the day and barbeques and entertainment on summer evenings. Most of the bedrooms are around a gallery hallway reached up a stone staircase off the entryway. They vary in size and, accordingly, price. All are modestly decorated with regional wood furniture, but they manage to preserve some original 19th-century charm due to the unusually high, molded ceilings, hardwood floors and tall windows. Our particular favorite is #11, an airy, green and white corner room. The double room reached through the restaurant downstairs is probably the best of them all - it's extra-large, quaintly decorated and has a spacious bath - but remember its location is a noisy one.

CASA DE LUMENA
Praca Alexandre Herculano, 27
8000 Faro, Portugal
tel: 89-22028
12 rooms - Inexpensive
Credit cards: all major
Restaurant
Nearest airport: Faro (8 km)
Nearest train station: Faro (1 km)

Six kilometers west of the busy seaside resort of Albufeira, overlooking an unspoiled stretch of sand called Praia de Gale, and surrounded by craggy cliffs, green hills and several top-notch golf courses, is the Vila Joya.   This Moorish fantasy of a hotel, opened in 1979, is the realized dream of Claudia Jung, a German who strives to make this the most exclusive and luxurious hostelry on the Algarve.   Its price and relatively isolated location practically guarantee its exclusivity, and this combination, together with a heated oval swimming pool, meticulous service and fine French cuisine, is an unbeatable recipe for those to whom money is no object.   Breakfast and dinner are included with the room rate. The dining room is lovely and intimate with a vaulted brick ceiling and open fireplace.   The Vila Joya is unique and opulent: staff attire is reminiscent of the "Arabian Nights", as is the bedroom decor, whose contemporary sleekness is accented with throw pillows, shag rugs, dazzling-white alcoves and ornately tiled baths.   A minimum of a week's stay is required during high season, and overnights are discouraged at any time, but a peaceful, carefree and memorable vacation is ensured.

VILA JOYA
Apartado 120
8200 Albufeira, Portugal
tel: 89-54795 telex: 56222
14 rooms - Very expensive
Closed: November 16 to December 19
Credit cards: none
Restaurant, Quiet setting, Pool
Nearest airport: Faro (38 km)
Nearest train station: Algoz (5 km)

This pousada, installed in a renovated 16th-century manor house, faces the cathedral in the heart of historic Guimaraes, surrounded by narrow streets and stone-paved plazas.   The main entrance is to the side of the house, through the original granite-block-framed doorway and into the cozy wood-beamed and red-tiled reception area.   The small inn is faithfully restored, and the reception sets the tone for the decor throughout.   The atmosphere is intimate and homey, with low, wood ceilings and antiques lending authenticity to the feeling of going back several centuries in time.   On the main floor are two sitting areas, a small bar and a charming restaurant which looks onto the cathedral square.   The bedrooms are found on the two upper floors, each with a tiny lounge at the far end of the hall.   The rooms have gleaming, dark hardwood floors and ceilings.   The simple, regional-style furniture is of a natural wood, complemented by woven spreads, drapes and rugs in natural colors.   Wood-framed windows overlook the colorful, medieval streets lined with stone houses and flower-draped iron and wood balconies.   If you're seeking comfort and historical ambiance in a central location, this pousada has it all.

POUSADA DE NOSSA SENHORA DA OLIVEIRA
Largo de Oliveira
4800 Guimaraes, Portugal
Tel: 53-412157 telex: 32875
16 rooms - Moderate
Credit cards: all major
Restaurant, 16th-century building
U.S. Rep: Marketing Ahead
Rep. tel: (212) 686-9213
Nearest airport: Porto (54 km)
Nearest train station: Guimaraes

This recently opened pousada is splendidly installed in the 12th-century convent of Santa Marinha da Costa, surrounded by park and gardens. The whitewashed and restored convent building is flanked on one side by a beautiful stone church, and on the other by a new wing of rooms, carefully constructed to retain the atmosphere of the original, whose 24 guestrooms were at one time cells for 48 nuns. The decor in the public rooms is an exciting blend of genuine antique and classy contemporary and results in elegant harmony. You can see one premeditated concession to history in the portions of original stone wall that have been left exposed here and there, and the wonderful stone pillars, arches and carved wood ceilings remain. The open interior cloister with its playing stone fountain now serves in warm weather as a delightful bar. The bedrooms have polished wood floors and high ceilings, and are richly decorated with pale, modern furniture and heavy, woven, cream-colored spreads. Those in the original convent have small stone-framed windows and walls thick enough for window seats. But the rooms in the new wing are more spacious and have wood-framed picture windows, raised sitting areas and large blue-and-white tiled baths. They all overlook either the city or the convent gardens.

POUSADA DE SANTA MARINHA DA COSTA
4800 Guimaraes, Portugal
Tel: 53-418453 telex: 32686
56 rooms - Expensive
Credit cards: all major
Restaurant, 12th-century convent
U.S. Rep: Marketing Ahead
Rep. tel: (212) 686-9213
Nearest airport: Porto (54 km)
Nearest train station: Guimaraes

This little gem, in the colorful fishing town of Lagos, is an excellent budget choice on the often expensive Algarve.   Its location in the heart of town makes it ideal for exploring Lagos on foot - it's just a few blocks from the main network of restaurants, bars and boutiques - but also makes it a trial to find and park nearby (we stopped in front just long enough to unload our luggage before going in search of parking).   The rose-colored manor dates back to the 18th century, and was converted to an albergaria in 1966.   Winding tile-and-stone stairways access the rambling hallways of the multi-leveled house, off   which are found intriguingly decorated bedrooms - no two remotely alike.   They have names instead of numbers and crowd a smattering of antiques into their diminutive dimensions.   (There is one suite, most often used for four people.) Spaciousness they cannot claim, but for color they are hard to beat.   For example, we had the blue-and-white "Romantico", the topmost room with steeply slanted ceiling, painted-iron twin beds, marble-topped dressing and side tables and an L-shaped three-level bathroom.   A special and welcome feature is the sunny, interior stone patio, sporting bougainvillea and a fountain, just outside the cozy lounge with its fireplace and tiny, gleaming bar.

CAZA DE SAO GONCALO
Rua Candido dos Reis, 73
8600 Lagos, Portugal
tel: 08-62171 telex: 57411
13 rooms - Inexpensive
Credit cards: all major
Open: April to October
18th-century manor house
Nearest airport: Faro (80 km)
Nearest train station: Lagos

The dramatically terraced, wine-producing region flanking the Douro River is famous for its scenery, but not well-known for inviting accommodation. The tiny Lamego Inn, situated on a lush green hillside overlooking the pretty little town of the same name, has recently undergone interior renovation (when we were there it was awaiting only exterior paint), and offers plain, pleasant lodging in an area of the country that should not be missed. Once a private villa, the small, cream-colored stucco building has a flat rooftop - ideal for sunning - and bright red shutters. The surrounding countryside is carpeted with vineyards and dotted with pine trees, and the tranquil back garden, highlighted with a central, square fountain and umbrella tables, commands a beautiful view of Lamego. The inn is located near the lovely Nossa Senhora de Remedios nature park and right next door to the Raposeira champagne adega, both of which should be visited while you are there. The interior consists of a small sitting room with stone hearth, a tiny corner bar, a spacious, attractive and reasonable dining room with a panoramic view, and seven high-ceilinged bedrooms with tiled baths. The rooms vary in price according to size (though all are within budget range), and are simply and comfortably furnished in dark wood, the beds topped with earth-tone chenille spreads.

ESTALAGEM DE LAMEGO
Estrada N2
5100 Lamego, Portugal
tel: 54-62162
7 rooms - Budget
Credit cards: MC, V
Restaurant
Nearest airport: Porto (155 km)
Nearest train station: Peso da Regua (15 km)

The Principe Real, centrally located atop one of the seven hills that make up the capital city, is a smart choice for those seeking a small hotel offering personalized service, convenience and comfort.   It's within walking distance of well-known Liberty Avenue as well as the main Praca do Comercio.   The lobby has a pretty blue-and-white tiled mural of Lisbon and a lovely lounge area with stone fireplace and deep, soft furniture.   Off the lounge is found an intimate, wood-panelled bar.   The bedrooms are upstairs and, with the exception of #4 on each floor, they are quite small.   The larger doubles are on the street side of the hotel, meaning they'll be a bit noisier, but if the tradeoff for more space is worth it to you, be sure to request one of these.   The high-ceilinged rooms have diminutive baths and balconies, those in back overlooking the stone courtyard and surrounding residences.   They are carpeted, with old-fashioned wood furniture and bright, flowery spreads and curtains.   On the top floor is a charming breakfast room, with red-tile floor, wood-beamed ceiling and smiling staff.   It has a wonderful view over the city rooftops all the way to the Sao Jorge castle on a distant hill.   For dinner you might try the Marcia Condessa restaurant just down the street featuring fado entertainment.

HOTEL PRINCIPE REAL
Rua da Alegria, 53
1200 Lisbon, Portugal
tel: 1-360116
24 rooms - Moderate
Credit cards: all major
U.S. Rep: Tourex
Rep. tel: (212) 635-0525
Nearest airport: Lisbon
Nearest train station: Lisbon

The York House is a delightful hotel in a city not noted for appealing hotels.   It fairly exudes charm, from the moment you ascend its stone-paved interior stairway flanked by ivy-covered walls, to the last friendly smile on your departure.   In between, you'll be treated to the hospitality that has been the York's trademark for over a hundred years.   Originally a 16th-century monastery, the York House became the barracks of the Royal Guards when the Marquis of Pombal dissolved the monastic order.   Since 1876, it has known French, British and, currently, Portuguese ownership.   You traverse a delightful interior garden patio - in refreshing contrast to the noisy street outside - to enter the hotel proper where, somewhere off a maze of antique-lined hallways, a very special bedroom awaits.   Each bedroom varies in size and shape, and authentic furnishings lovingly preserve an old-world atmosphere. The enchanting dining room overlooks the patio with its flowery vines, and serves hearty and creative set meals.   A further seventeen spacious, handsome bedrooms in the annex across the street are decorated in opulent Victorian decor.   The York House is a popular oasis, so be sure to make advance reservations.

YORK HOUSE
Rua das Janelas Verdes, 32
1200 Lisbon, Portugal
tel: 1-662544
68 rooms - Expensive
Credit cards: all major
Restaurant, Quiet city location
Nearest airport: Lisbon
Nearest train station: Lisbon

Thirteen switchbacked kilometers straight up from the picturesque red-and-whitewashed village of Manteigas, in the heart of the dramatic Serra da Estrela, is perched this rustic mountain inn.   Constructed in the 1940s of native stone, with a multi-level red-tile roof, the pousada most resembles a ski-lodge and, indeed, the sport is pursued in the nearby Penhas da Saude.   Fishing and hiking are also popular, due to the proximity of the Mondego River and the beautiful Vale do Rossim lake.   The accommodations are simple and comfortable.   The spotless, whitewashed bedrooms are small, but attractively furnished with pale-wood four-poster twin beds.   The second-floor rooms have tiny terraces with breathtaking views over the terraced, green mountainsides to the village below, while the main-floor rooms have windows overlooking the valley, but their vistas are not so encompassing.   A pitched cathedral ceiling of gleaming wood caps the comfy foyer/lounge downstairs and the cozy, wood-panelled television room upstairs, which has deep, dark sofas and a masonry hearth.   An open, central fireplace warms the dining room, locally known for its regional specialties and the fabulous panoramic view.

POUSADA DE SAO LOURENCO
Estrada de Gouveia
6260 Manteigas, Portugal
tel: 75-47150 telex: 53992
14 rooms - Moderate
Credit cards: all major
Restaurant, Dramatic views
U.S. Rep: Marketing Ahead
Rep. tel: (212) 686-9213
Nearest airport: Porto (300 km)
Nearest train station: Belmonte (30 km)

Together with similar vantage points up and down the border, the hilltop town of Marvao, only six kilometers from Spain, was ringed with fortifications in the 14th century by King Dom Dinis.   As you approach the village, rising like a fist from the Alentejo plains, it appears impregnable still.   Within its ramparts is a sleepy pousada that, for over 40 years, has been offering travellers comfort, tranquility and good food in one of the most dramatic settings in the country. Within, the decor imparts the flavor of a simple mountain lodge: the cozy lounge and restaurant have brick-red tile floors, wood-beamed sloped ceilings and stone-and-azulejo fireplaces.   The piece de resistance is the glassed-in terrace shared by the bar and restaurant, whose interesting regional menu includes a variety of game dishes.   The endless panorama takes your breath away, stretching across the Serra de Marvao and into Spain.   Be sure to request one of the rooms that shares that view (five more are being added), a few of which have small terraces.   The others (slightly larger) overlook the narrow, cobblestone street.   The rooms are small, plain and pleasant, with wood-tile floors, dark, regional-style furniture, high, whitewashed ceilings and flowery bedspreads.

POUSADA DE SANTA MARIA
Rua 24 de Janeiro, 7
7330 Marvao, Portugal
tel: 45-93201 telex: 42360
13 rooms - Moderate
Credit cards: all major
Restaurant, mountain setting
U.S. Rep: Marketing Ahead
Rep tel: (212) 686-9213
Nearest airport: Lisbon (230 km)
Nearest train station: Marvao (10 km)

This roadside inn is appropriately called "Mountain Shelter", since it is tucked against a mountainside, shaded by trees, and overlooks the breathtaking sierra of Monchique and, on a clear day, beyond to the sea. It is located just a few kilometers from the quaint mountain village of Monchique, known for its brass and woven wool handicrafts, and only 25 kilometers from the beach and bustling Algarve, making it an ideal spot for those travellers seeking tranquility without sacrificing convenience. Broad stone stairs lead up to a wide terrace which runs the length of this modern building. Here you can enjoy lunch and the panoramic view of the valley below. Inside, the dining room has picture windows, a sunken fireplace and excellent regional cuisine (try the "asadura", a delectable specialty consisting of grilled pork, chopped and mixed with oil, garlic, lemon and cilantro, served over rice). The bedrooms upstairs are cozy, simply decorated with painted iron beds and flowery bedspreads. They all have spotless wood floors, cork ceilings and colorfully tiled bathrooms. For a surprisingly small additional sum you can occupy a suite that includes a small sitting room and fireplace. All the bedrooms share the unforgettable view.

ESTALAGEM ABRIGO DA MONTANHA
Estrada da Foia
8550 Monchique, Portugal
tel: 82-92131
8 rooms - Inexpensive
Credit cards: all major
Restaurant, Mountain setting
Nearest airport: Faro (81 km)
Nearest train station: Portimao (25 km)

Mons Cicus, the Latin derivate for Monchique, is a tranquil, luxurious hideaway on the road between the market town of Monchique and Foia peak.   Tourists flock to Foia for the same view available from the hotel's terrace: over the green hills of the Serra de Monchique to the town of Portimao and beyond to the Atlantic.   Built as a private home about 25 years ago, it is currently under meticulous French ownership.   The dazzling-white structure is tucked against a forested hillside, has royal-blue shutters, terracotta-tiled roof and is fronted by an expanse of green lawn which has two pools, a tennis court and a sauna.   The wood-beamed restaurant and bar on the main floor are charming, with marble floors and open fireplaces.   Upstairs, there are three bedrooms in the original house and five in a newer addition, all of which are spacious and simply elegant. They are carpeted in soft colors, decorated in beige, blue or yellow and white, have high ceilings and handsome wood furniture.   The high wood beds with their tapestry-like spreads are striking.   The older rooms all have terraces and cavernous marble baths.   Blue-and-white #3 has the largest terrace (even the bathroom has one), and is our favorite.   The few rooms without terrace are more economical, but none is expensive, and a view is worth every additional escudo.   Mons Cicus offers a wonderful retreat into self-indulgence.

HOTEL MONS CICUS
Estrada da Foia
8550 Monchique, Portugal
tel: 82-92650 telex: 58362
8 rooms - Inexpensive
Credit cards: all major
Restaurant, Pools, Tennis
Nearest airport: Faro (81 km)
Nearest train station: Portimao (25 km)

In the 14th century, King Dom Dinis had massive fortifications built around the tiny towns on the border with Spain to protect Portugal from that country's aggression.   The hilltop town of Monsaraz was one of these, and its walls still stand as testimony to the King's successful strategy.   But the heyday of threatened conflict is past, and Monsaraz is now just a picturesque, sleepy, cobblestoned village.   But if tranquility, dramatic setting and traditional atmosphere are your cup of tea, this estalagem in the heart of town off a peaceful stone-paved square, offers an ideal overnight stop for a bargain-basement price.   Though constructed in 1970, the whitewashed inn, with its bright-blue-painted cornerstones, green door, red terracotta roof and stone-framed windows, looks outside and in like a century-old house.   All is dark and cozy within; low stone doorways lead to the red-tiled, wood-beamed lounge and spotless restaurant, both with whitewashed, open stone fireplaces.   The bedrooms are up the back stairs through heavy wooden doors and overlook the surrounding countryside.   They are furnished in plain, carved regional wood, the beds topped with rough woven spreads.   In back is a garden terrace with tables and chairs, and a pool.

ESTALAGEM DE MONSARAZ
Largo de Sao Bartolomeu
7200 Monsaraz, Portugal
tel: 66-55112
7 rooms - Budget
Credit cards: all major
Restaurant, Pool, Medieval atmosphere
Nearest airport: Lisbon (200 km)
Nearest train station: Reguengos de Monsaraz (17 km)

The Atlantic stretches a long finger of water inland at Aveiro, and it is after this inlet, or "ria", that the pousada is named. Though one of the earlier entries in the pousada network, the small wood-and-stone inn has a modern flavor within and without. It is built smack on the water's edge, so briny sea air and the sound of gently lapping waves are constant company. Its isolated location, between Sao Jacinto and Torreira on the opposite shore of the ria from Aveiro, ensure peace and quiet. The multi-leveled, expansive lounge and lobby are sleek and shiny. The restaurant, well-reputed for its seafood dishes, is decorated in cool green and white with wood and leather furniture. Sliding glass doors lead from the dining room to a long, sunny outdoor terrace over the water, where colorful boats glide by bearing the products of the ria: salt, algae and fish. All of the bedrooms share the view of the calm, blue inlet from balconies just large enough for a breakfast table. The rooms are neither spacious nor luxurious, but are comfortably and simply furnished in blonde, wicker-like wood and accented with flower-print spreads and drapes. The Pousada da Ria offers a tranquil refuge for a day or two while exploring the surrounding area.

POUSADA DA RIA
Bico do Muranzel - Torreira
3870 Murtosa, Portugal
tel: 34-48332 telex: 37061
19 rooms - Moderate
Credit cards: all major
Restaurant, Pool
U.S. Rep: Marketing Ahead
Rep. tel: (212) 686-9213
Nearest airport: Porto (60 km)
Nearest train station: Ovar (20 km)

The enchanting hilltop white town of Obidos rises from the plains and is crowned by a 13th-century castle built by King Dom Dinis.   In the 15th century a palace was installed within the castle walls, but in 1755 both palace and castle were severely damaged by an earthquake.   After extensive restoration, a pousada now stands on the site of the ruined palace, surrounded by ancient ramparts interspersed with dramatic crenellated towers.   Well-marked parking is outside the castle walls; from there follow an interior stone courtyard to check in and send someone back for your luggage.   The public rooms are distinctly medieval in decor, with high stone ceilings, burnished red-tile floors and dark antiques – even a suit of armor.   On the main floor are a wood-beamed lounge and bar with worn, comfortable armchairs, and upstairs are both another sitting room with open stone fireplace and the elegant dining room overlooking the courtyard through arched, stone-framed windows.   Narrow hallways lead to six small, wood-ceilinged bedrooms with surprisingly uninspired furnishings, the beds topped with brightly flowered spreads.   However, the three suites, installed in the dark rampart towers, are richly decorated with antiques and loaded with historical ambiance, but expensive with inconvenient floorplans.

POUSADA DO CASTELO
Paco Real, 2510 Obidos, Portugal
tel: 62-95105 telex 15540
9 rooms - Expensive
Credit cards: all major
Restaurant, 13th-century castle
U.S. Rep: Marketing Ahead
Rep. tel: (212) 686-9213
Nearest airport: Lisbon (80 km)
Nearest train station: Obidos

Our favorite hotel in medieval Obidos, this inn was originally an early 19th-century convent, converted in the 20th century to a modest hostelry, then carefully refurbished by its current owner in 1978. It enjoys a relatively peaceful street-front location slightly removed from, but within easy walking distance of, the center of town. It also boasts the only really good restaurant in Obidos, whose charming decor - heavy wood-beamed ceiling, red-tile floor and open stone fireplace - promises a pleasurable dining experience whether or not you are a guest in the hotel. Ten bedrooms are being added to the existing 13, and should be completed by fall of 1986. Several of these new rooms will have fabulous views of the city and castle. Although every room guarantees traditional flavor, only five are found in the original convent building; their beautifully preserved wood ceilings and unusual dimensions making them the most appealing. All of the bedrooms have high ceilings, textured whitewashed walls, tile floors, painted wrought-iron beds and traditional dark-wood furniture. There is a sitting room upstairs with fireplace, two cozy bars (one open to the public, one for hotel guests only), and an interior garden patio where guests can dine in fine weather. For simple, old-fashioned comfort, this inn offers an exceptional value.

ESTALAGEM DO CONVENTO
Rua Dom Joao de Ornelas
2510 Obidos, Portugal
tel: 62-95214 telex: 44906   95217
13 rooms - Inexpensive
Credit cards: MC, VS
Restaurant
Nearest airport: Lisbon (80 km)
Nearest train station: Obidos

This roadside inn (built in 1950) occupies the former site of a "quinta", or farm, within sight of the enchanting hilltop town of Obidos. The large whitewashed and red-roofed building is set back from the main road (N8) just north of town, and is flanked on one side by a circular stone tower which houses a bar/lounge on its upper two levels and a tiny stone-walled discotheque in the basement. The accommodations here are simple, but not ordinary. The larger-than-average bedrooms - each slightly different - have high ceilings, regional-style wood furniture and colorful bedspreads, offering noteworthy comfort (and an occasional crack in their whitewashed walls) for their modest price. Pretty, hand-painted wood ceilings grace the big, sunny breakfast room (there is no restaurant) and the spacious lounge. There is also a homey little sitting/television room off which extends a nice esplanade where you can relax on a hot afternoon or warm evening. Thanks to its countrified setting, the Mansao da Torre is able to offer such attractive features as two swimming pools, tennis court and a garden with children's playground, yet you're still within walking distance of medieval Obidos, and a short drive from Caldas da Rainha.

MANSAO DA TORRE
Casal do Zambujeiro
2510 Obidos, Portugal
tel: 62-95247
12 rooms - Budget
Credit cards: all major
Pools, Rural setting
Nearest airport: Lisbon (75 km)
Nearest train station: Caldas da Rainha (3 km)

This is a spanking-new (1985) whitewashed and iron-balconied inn in the heart of medieval Obidos. It fronts the stone-paved Rua Direita, the main street in town, which is lined with art galleries and souvenir shops, and leads up to the castle. Along with the obvious advantages of its central location comes the inconvenience of parking. (You'll need to stop just long enough to unload your luggage before going in search of a parking place on a side street.) The hotel occupies the site of a former private residence which had fallen into disrepair. The owner rebuilt from the ground up, creating modern comfort while recreating a traditional ambiance throughout. The handsome public rooms are furnished in wood and leather and plentifully accented with colorful painted tiles. There are two attractive bars - one for the general public and the other for hotel guests only. Breakfast is the only meal served. The bedrooms vary in price according to location, decor and plumbing (bathtub or shower), but all are approximately the same size, have whitewashed walls, regional-style wood furniture, flowery spreads and drapes and brightly tiled baths. To us, bedroom location seemed inconsequential - overlooking old stone ramparts in back, narrow side streets, or the Rua Direita seemed equally appealing - but the corner doubles (at double the price) with wood-beamed ceilings are definitely more charming.

ALBERGARIA RAINHA SANTA ISABEL
Rua Direita
2510 Obidos, Portugal
tel: 62-95115
20 rooms - Inexpensive
Credit cards: all major
Central location
Nearest airport: Lisbon (80 km)
Nearest train station: Obidos

This sparkling-white pousada is one of the youngest and most dramatic of the government's hotels. Installed in a 15th-century monastery commissioned by King Joao I, and facing Palmela's enchanting castle, this "inn" is the essence of austere elegance and serenity. Verdant cultivated countryside surrounds its hilltop setting, guaranteeing panoramic vistas from every room. Inside, the focal point of the pousada is its sun-drenched central cloister, enclosed by a symmetrical parade of stone arches. Light falls through the arcade onto broad, pale-stone hallways beneath vaulted ceilings, furnished with natural leather armchairs for lounging. Upstairs are found the large, airy bedrooms, their decor a perfect mingling of old and modern. The floors are richly tiled in wine-red, the deep stone windows wood-framed and shuttered. The bedspreads and floor-to-ceiling drapes are cream-colored with subdued earth-tone accents, and woven from rough native material. A low-slung, soft-leather armchair and simple, regional wood furniture round out the picture of comfort. The spacious bathrooms are colorfully tiled and spotless. As for dining, the kitchen here has established a reputation for its fine regional cuisine.

POUSADA CASTELO DE PALMELA
2950 Palmela, Portugal
tel: 1-2351226 telex: 42290
27 rooms - Expensive
Credit cards: all major
Restaurant, Medieval building
U.S. Rep: Marketing Ahead
Rep. tel: (212) 686-9213
Nearest airport: Lisbon (38 km)
Nearest train station: Palmela (7 km)

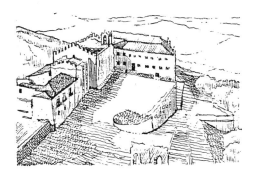

This handsome estate dates back to the 17th century, when its history was entwined through a scandalous marriage with that of the nearby Paco de Calheiros, also a guest house. Since then, the property has changed hands several times, currently being owned and occupied by three elderly sisters of the Pimenta Lopes family, whose uncle acquired it in 1917. A tiny sign about a kilometer outside Ponte de Lima on the way to Ponte da Barca points across the road to the stone and whitewashed farmhouse - recently and faithfully restored. There are four bedrooms with bath on the main floor - two large (ask for the big one at the back, it's worth the few dollars more), and two somewhat smaller, but each charming in its simplicity. The walls and threshholds are thick stone, the wood floors creaky, the ceilings high and the furnishings a variety of plain, handsome antiques. A beautiful wood staircase, under a cathedral-ceiling skylight, leads upstairs to a gallery and six additional bedrooms under the eaves. These are quaint and offer an interesting budget option, but they are also tiny and share a hallway bath. The dining room (which will prepare dinner if there's a full house) has one long table, a fireplace at one end, and a marvelous old kitchen with a stone oven and open hearth at the other. The setting is bucolic, but just moments from historic Ponte de Lima.

CASA DE CRASTO
4990 Ponte de Lima, Portugal
tel: 58-961156
10 rooms - Inexpensive
Credit cards: none
Private manor house
Nearest airport: Porto (93 km)
Nearest train station: Viana do Castelo (23 km)

Just south of Portimao is Praia da Rocha, an expanse of broad beach flanked by the rocky cliffs so ubiquitous in the Algarve. At the east end of the beach, opposite a stone fortress and across the street from the sea, is the Vila Lido. Jacqueline Kennedy was a guest here before the private villa was converted into an inn 15 years ago. Like so many structures in the south, the turquoise-shuttered house is whitewashed, with the carved chimneys, so characteristic of the region, jutting from its red-tile roof. A low stone-and-plaster wall surrounds the property and broad stone steps lead to the arched entryway where a tiny plaque gives the only indication that this is other than a private residence. Inside, the albergaria is meticulously cared for, the public rooms a delight. A sunny sitting room with polished parquet floors gives onto a verandah at the front of the house, both ideal for coffee or cocktails while sea-gazing. French doors lead from there into a charming breakfast room with hand-painted walls, carved ceiling, massive fireplace and delicate furniture. A few of the bedrooms have decorative fireplaces, and all retain a genuine old-world flavor with their sculpted ceilings, tall windows, spacious dimensions and solid chestnut doors, but the furnishings are relatively modern and uninspired. #21, #22 and #25 have terraces, the latter room being the largest and slightly more expensive.

ALBERGARIA VILA LIDO
Praia da Rocha
8500 Portimao, Portugal
tel: 82-24127
10 rooms - Inexpensive
Credit cards: all major
Across street from beach
Nearest airport: Faro (64 km)
Nearest train station: Portimao (2 km)

This luxurious hotel is a haven in the heart of Portugal's second city. Originally built in 1951 by textile magnate Fernando de Sousa to accommodate his foreign customers, it has since been elegantly converted to a hotel, still owned by the well-known businessman, and a showcase for some of the antiques and tapestries he has collected over the years. The style is grand, with large, plush public rooms, a gracefully carved staircase overseen by stained glass, wide hallways and high sculpted ceilings. The atmosphere is old-world intimate, the dining room fine and the service unparalleled. The attention to detail is remarkable, as can be noted in the gleaming woodwork, the velvet settee in the elevator and the charming small bar with its curious original ceiling depicting the towns of Portugal. The bedrooms are generously proportioned, with high, scalloped ceilings, and each features television and minibar. All are richly furnished with handsome wood pieces, and are decorated in soft brown and white. You may choose to overlook the rooftops of Porto (request a top floor away from street noise), or the colorful courtyard solarium. (The owner's son added forty-four bedrooms to the original count; these are similar in decor, somewhat smaller and slightly less expensive.)

HOTEL INFANTE DE SAGRES
Praca D. Filipa de Lencastre, 62
4000 Porto, Portugal
tel: 2-28101 telex: 26880
84 rooms - Moderate
Credit cards: all major
Restaurant, Central location
Nearest airport: Porto (15 km)
Nearest train station: Porto (2 km)

Located within hailing distance of Cabo Sao Vicente (the most southwesterly point in Europe) is a tiny stone fortress.   Careful inspection of a carved stone over the entryway reveals the number 1632 - the date it was constructed. Perched on a rocky promontory overlooking the craggy coast and the sea, it offers only four guestrooms, most of its traffic a result of its restaurant's reputation.   The original fortress walls enclose two whitewashed buildings, one housing the reception, a small bar and the cozy dining room, which has a lovely wood ceiling.   The other contains whitewashed bedrooms with brick-red tile floors and large baths.   They vary only slightly: each is comfortably sized and simply appointed with regional dark-wood furniture and pale bedspreads.   One bedroom has a clear view of the ocean while the others look onto the seaside terrace or into the interior garden, which is graced by a little white chapel.   The dramatic setting is ideal for those seeking tranquility, but is still readily accessible for touring the Algarve.   Best of all, it's only about half the price of its pousada neighbor (indeed, the Pousada do Infante books its overflow here).

CASA DE CHA DA FORTALEZA DO BELICHE
8650 Sagres,
Portugal
tel: 82-64124
4 rooms - Inexpensive
Credit cards: none
Restaurant, Romantic setting
Nearest airport: Faro (100 km)
Nearest train station: Lagos (35 km)

Sagres, on the relatively untamed western edge of the famous Algarve coast, has a sophisticated pousada, well situated to take advantage of the view. Overlooking the merging waters of the Mediterranean Sea and the Atlantic Ocean, the Infante (named after Prince Henry the Navigator) is a large whitewashed, red-roofed structure providing serenity and comfort in a comparatively isolated location, while still offering easy access to the highlights of the popular resort areas - such as long beaches, hidden coves and fishing villages. The clifftop hotel, built in 1960, has a Moorish flavor and has been recently remodelled, with excellent results. Giving onto a grassy terrace which extends to the sea is a spacious tiled lounge, with a large fireplace and cozy furniture, tastefully decorated in greens and browns. In addition to good food, the dining room has a fireplace, an arched ceiling and colorful tiles that climb halfway up the walls. The bedrooms are carpeted and fairly roomy, with regional wood furnishings and flowery bedspreads. They are not opulent, but they are newly refurbished and very pleasant; plus all have views of the sea and rocky coast. Several bedrooms have balconies (at no extra cost), so be sure to ask if one of these is available.

POUSADA DO INFANTE
8650 Sagres, Portugal
tel: 82-64222 telex: 57491
23 rooms - Expensive
Credit cards: all major
Restaurant, Sea views
U.S. Rep: Marketing Ahead
Rep. tel: (212) 686-9213
Nearest airport: Faro (100 km)
Nearest train station: Lagos (35 km)

We are not the only ones to find the Reserve a special place: it is the only Portuguese member of the discriminating "Relais & Chateaux" and boasts a restaurant that merits three Michelin red forks. Nestled in the hills above Faro, and cushioned by six acres of private property (which includes a tennis court), peace and quiet is prized at this exclusive retreat, yet championship golf courses, horseback riding, sandy beaches, and the largest resort area on the Algarve are located within fifteen kilometers. Reservations are strongly recommended at the splendid restaurant which is closed on Tuesdays. The Swiss owners built a twenty-suite hotel on the grounds in 1982. These are either one- or two-bedroom, with a corresponding number of large and lovely bathrooms. Each features an equipped kitchenette, stocked bar, refrigerator, and a wide terrace overlooking the immaculate lawn, the beautiful swimming pool and the sea. The rooms are decorated in modern Mediterranean: cool blue and sparkling white, with deep, comfy couch and chairs, glass-topped tables, wrought-iron beds and charming corner fireplace. As you might expect, such luxury, enhanced by impeccable service, is not for the budget-conscious.

HOTEL LA RESERVE
Santa Barbara de Nexe
Algarve, Portugal
tel: 89-91234 telex: 56790
20 suites - Very expensive
Credit cards: none
Restaurant, Pool, Good views
U.S. Rep: D. B. Mitchell
Rep. tel: (212) 696-1323
Nearest airport: Faro (10 km)
Nearest train station: Faro (10 km)

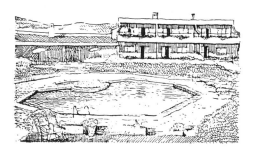

Constructed in 1945, this small rose-colored and ivy-covered pousada was one of the first in Portugal, and still maintains the flavor of a "wayside" inn, ideally situated for an overnight on your way between Lisbon and the southern coast. From its flowering back garden, featuring terrace and pool, is a captivating view of Santiago do Cacem with its hilltop castle, and the ruins of the Roman town of Mirobriga are just a few minutes away by car. The atmosphere throughout is country-cozy, the regional wood furnishings dating from the time of construction. The rustic whitewashed bedrooms are small but spotless, as are the baths, and have hardwood floors and carved wood beds with flowered spreads. There are four rooms in the original building (our favorites), and three in an annex behind. The views are either toward town or overlooking the tranquil, verdant countryside. The dining room is warm and inviting, with a beamed ceiling, red-tile floor, crockery displayed over the doors and windows, and a sunken conversation pit facing a tiled fireplace where guests take coffee or cocktails. The meals are hearty, tasty and reasonable, regional specialties being the mainstay of the menu. The staff is especially welcoming.

POUSADA DE SAO TIAGO
Estrada de Lisboa
7540 Santiago do Cacem, Portugal
tel: 69-22459 telex: 11166
7 rooms - Moderate
Credit cards: DC, VS
Restaurant, Pool, Lovely setting
U.S. Rep: Marketing Ahead
Rep. tel: (212) 686-9213
Nearest airport: Lisbon (140 km)
Nearest train station: Santiago do Cacem (1 km)

Three kilometers above the village of Sao Bras is one of Portugal's earliest pousadas: built in 1943 with six rooms, it typified the small wayside inn which paved the way for the more elegant pousadas of today. Resembling a whitewashed manor house with red terracotta roof, it retains the flavor of a roadside inn, offering travellers a peaceful spot, removed from the heavily travelled coastal route, but still readily accessible to its activities. The pousada is surrounded by pine and eucalyptus and its bedrooms all have balconies and enjoy views overlooking Sao Bras, Faro and the Atlantic in the distance. The rooms are simple, whitewashed, almost stark, with dark, heavy-wood furniture, marble-topped dressers and end tables, white bedspreads and wood floors. The public rooms are cozy and rustic. The wood-beamed lounge/bar features an open glazed-brick fireplace, deep leather furniture and throw rugs on rough-hewn wood floors. The semicircular restaurant is locally popular, and has lovely views over the garden terrace and the countryside from its window tables. The Sao Bras provides an excellent base for excursions to the market town of Loule, the charming white town of Montes Novos and the ruins of Milreu.

POUSADA DE SAO BRAS
8150 Sao Bras de Alportel
Algarve, Portugal
tel: 89-42305 telex: 56945
23 rooms - Moderate
Credit cards: all major
Restaurant, Country setting
U.S. Rep: Marketing Ahead
Rep. tel: (212) 686-9213
Nearest airport: Faro (20 km)
Nearest train station: Loule (17 km)

The picturesque coastal village of Sao Martinho, with its half-moon bay ringed with rocky cliffs, is an appealing destination for those seeking peace and quiet in a quaint setting.   It has the additional attraction of offering a convenient base for excursions to nearby Obidos and Alcobaca.   Its small semicircular beach is clean and looks over calm water dotted with colorful fishing boats.   The Hotel Parque is just a block from the bay on a shady, tree-lined street.   Originally an elegant turn-of-the-century manor, the red-roofed, cream-colored inn is accented with pretty pink and green azulejos outside, and is surrounded by luxuriant gardens featuring a tennis court.   Inside, the large and lovely public rooms are well-maintained and -furnished with period pieces.   A broad hallway leads to spacious double rooms and a huge suite, all with 15-foot sculpted ceilings, tall windows overlooking the gardens and handsome furniture in traditional Portuguese style.   We recommend you secure one of these charming lower-floor (planta baixa) rooms, since those upstairs are small, with low ceilings and utilitarian furniture.   Not all have full baths, and some none at all, sharing hallway facilities.   But they are clean and carry a shoestring pricetag.

HOTEL PARQUE
Avenida Marechal Carmona, 3
Sao Martinho do Porto, Portugal
tel: 62-98505
34 rooms - Budget
Credit cards: all major
Open: March to November
Tennis
Nearest airport: Lisbon (108 km)
Nearest train station: Sao Martinho do Porto

Imagine our surprise when, out of curiosity, we followed accommodation signs out of Tomar, through the village of Serra, and ended up at a small stone building on the shore of a lake with no more road to follow. Taking our next cue from an arrow, we went down a flight of stairs to find a small bar and a dock. When we inquired about the inn, we were informed that the boat was about to leave. It was then we noticed the small, pine-covered island in the middle of the broad blue lake and, on it, the inn. So we paid our 150 escudos (round trip) and took the launch to lunch. The whitewashed, red-roofed estalagem sits at one end of the island, wrapped around a large pool and grassy terrace. Through the airy reception area and upstairs is a cozy, rustic bar with a fireplace which leads to a bright, comfy lounge off the restaurant - all with wood-beamed ceilings and deep-red tile floors. The dining room offers good regional specialties and a lovely view across the lake. The bedrooms - all with lake views - are smallish and simply furnished in motel-modern style, with colorful flowered bedspreads. This is an ideal getaway spot offering nothing but peace and quiet, where you can unwind in the sun, or take a boat out fishing. The ferry goes between island and shore every hour until early evening.

ESTALAGEM DA ILHA DO LOMBO
2300 Serra de Tomar, Portugal
tel: 49-37128
15 rooms - Inexpensive
Credit cards: all major
Restaurant, Pool
Unique island setting
Nearest airport: Lisbon (170 km)
Nearest train station: Tomar (16 km)

This impressive pousada is installed in the Sao Filipe castle which towers above the town of Setubal and over the bay. Wind your way up to the towering structure, visible from afar, and leave your car outside the walls. From here, a wide, stone-paved stairway wends you past a tiny blue-and-white tiled chapel to the broad terrace where you'll find the reception area. Further flights of stone steps (there is no elevator) lead to the roomy, whitewashed bedrooms, with high ceilings and walls thick enough to accommodate window seats. Large baths, red-tile floors, traditional carved-wood furniture and earth-tone, floral-print spreads and drapes combine to create extremely comfortable surroundings with a somewhat rustic flavor. Unfortunately, not all of the rooms have a view of the city and the bay - which is enchanting - so be sure to request one. On the main level is a tiled lounge with well-worn, cozy furniture, a television and a small bar. The restaurant is especially appealing, overlooking the sunwashed terrace (where you can sit in warm weather) and the water. It is justifiably popular with locals and guests alike, specializing in superior regional cuisine.

POUSADA DE SAO FILIPE
Castelo de Sao Filipe
2900 Setubal, Portugal
tel: 65-23844
15 rooms - Expensive
Credit cards: all major
Restaurant, 16th-century castle
U.S. Rep: Marketing Ahead
Rep. tel: (212) 686-9213
Nearest airport: Lisbon (51 km)
Nearest train station: Setubal

The Palace of Seven Sighs, so-called due to a legendary and intricate love story involving a Portuguese nobleman and a Moorish princess, is a splendid example of late 18th-century architecture (it will celebrate its bicentennial in 1987). One of its several owners was the Marquis of Marialva, who authored Portuguese bullfighting rules. The elegant white-stone building is set amidst sculpted gardens and surrounded by expansive panoramas of the lush, emerald-green Sintra countryside. From the front lawn you can see the ornate Palacio de Pena on a hill above town. The grand-scale public rooms are nothing short of spectacular, decorated in pastel colors, with high, molded ceilings, hand-painted walls, wood or marble floors covered with oriental rugs, and abundant antiques topped by fresh-cut flowers. Each of the spacious bedrooms is unique, most twin-bedded, furnished mainly with richly upholstered period pieces, and decorated in muted earthtones. Bucolic views from tall windows complete the picture. The first-floor bedrooms have the added attraction of extra-high ceilings, augmenting their already generous proportions. There is a charming bar downstairs, an appealing awning-covered outdoor terrace, and the dining room offers quite good Continental cuisine.

HOTEL PALACIO DE SETEAIS
Rua Barbosa do Bocage, 8
2710 Sintra, Portugal
tel: 92-33200 telex: 14410
18 rooms - Very expensive
Credit cards: all major
Restaurant, 18th-century palace
Nearest airport: Lisbon (30 km)
Nearest train station: Sintra (3 km)

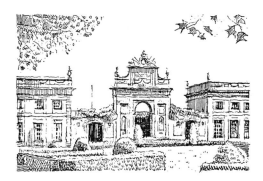

011-351-192-33200

To reach one of our favorite inns in Portugal, watch for a sign just east of Monserrate, and follow the rough narrow road until you can go no farther, then knock on the doors in the high wall to your left. A rest home for monks in the 16th century (ask to see the original chapel), it has been the family home of the Braddell family for the past fifty years, but a guest house for only a few. After undergoing extensive restoration and expansion, it has become a vacation spot of unsurpassed comfort, within driving distance of several weeks' worth of sightseeing if you can resist the immediate temptation of the appealing garden, swimming pool and the shady, clay tennis courts. The proprietor is English (his wife Spanish), and an avid collector of the antiques which abound throughout the house, in which you are free to roam at will. Every bedroom is different, furnished with delightful antiques and decorated with exquisite taste. The suites are a special treat - large and lovely - and, for the money, worth every escudo of the ten additional dollars charged. The family prides itself on personal service - from tailoring dinner to your taste, to helping you plan your itinerary during your stay and after. The Quinta has many loyal clients. Reservations at least three days in advance are a must.

QUINTA DE SÃO THIAGO
Monserrate
2710 Sintra, Portugal
tel:/-92-32923
10 rooms - Moderate
Credit cards: none
Private manor house, Pool
Nearest airport: Lisbon (25 km)
Nearest train station: Sintra (4 km)

This out-of-the-way inn is perched just above the Castelo de Bode hydroelectric dam on the Zezere River, beside a deep blue reservoir of the same name. Its dramatic natural setting - surrounded by olive- and pine-forested hills - attracts water-sports enthusiasts, offering such activities as waterskiing, sailing, motorboating and fishing. Originally built in 1945 to house the dam construction engineers, it was converted to a pousada in the early '50s. White-washed, green-shuttered and red-roofed, the Sao Pedro provides rustic comfort for road-weary travellers. The smallish, high-ceilinged bedrooms (six in a tree-shaded annex), are plain, but pleasant, with thin carpet, simple wood furniture and flowery drapes and spreads. Not all of the rooms look toward the reservoir; our favorite was a corner room which looks onto the water and the woods. A small bar downstairs opens onto an outdoor stone terrace with a good view of the dam. The wood and red-tiled sitting room is cozily furnished and features a stone fireplace, making it a gathering spot on cool mountain evenings. The green-and-white dining room is particularly pretty, and overlooks the reservoir through big picture windows.

POUSADA DE SAO PEDRO
Castelo de Bode
2300 Tomar, Portugal
tel: 49-38175 telex: 42392
15 rooms - Moderate
Credit cards: all major
Restaurant
U.S. Rep: Marketing Ahead
Rep. tel: (212) 686-9213
Nearest airport: Lisbon (150 km)
Nearest train station: Tomar (14 km)

Between the quaint little towns of Canas de Senhorim and Nelas, watch for a sign saying Urgeirica-Hotel, and to the left you'll see the large stone and whitewashed hotel surrounded by verdant grounds, in which you'll later discover tennis courts and a pool. Currently Portuguese-owned, it was originally built in the 1930s by a British mining engineer who owned the nearby uranium mines until they were nationalized. From within and without it has the appearance and ambiance of a rambling hunting lodge - offering simple comfort in a beautiful mountain setting at a budget price. The lounge and restaurant are spacious and subdued, with high ceilings, hardwood floors and solid, well-worn furniture. Located off meandering hallways are bigger-than-average bedrooms, each distinct and appointed with a pleasing mixture of regional-wood and antique furniture. We especially liked the high, old-fashioned beds common to all the rooms. There are a few special rooms (a couple with terraces) that are nearly twice the size and have parquet floors and elegant antique pianos converted into dressing tables. For less than $5 more, these are a real bargain if available (# 123 and # 124 are our favorites).   The cool mountain air and the spectacular Serra da Estrela nearby make the Hotel Urgeirica an appealing budget choice.

HOTEL URGEIRICA
Canas de Senhorim
3520 Nelas, Portugal
tel: 32-67267
53 rooms - Budget
Credit cards: all major
Restaurant, Pool, Tennis
Nearest airport: Porto (165 km)
Nearest train station: Canas de Senhorim (4 km)

The small town of Valenca do Minho hugs the banks of the Minho River which divides Portugal from Spain as it meanders its way to the sea.   The old part of town, within the walls of the fortaleza, has tiny, whitewashed houses huddled over narrow cobblestone streets and, on the water's edge, a pousada which looks across the river into Spain.   The public rooms are spotless and modern; the bright, airy lounge/bar and cozy, sunken conversation pit with open hearth are graced with deep leather furniture and entice you to linger over coffee or cocktails.   Off the lounge, flanked on two sides by floor-to-ceiling glass windows affording a smashing view, is another appealing sitting area with TV. The outdoor terrace features a fountain, and overlooks cool, green lawn and old stone walls which lead down to the riverbank.   The same dramatic panorama is shared by the good dining room, which has a wood ceiling and deep red rugs.   Nor does a single bedroom forego the view, although not all have terraces, so be sure to request one if available.   The guestrooms are without exception spacious (those with twin beds even more so), and have large, tiled baths, high ceilings, parquet floors and handcrafted, regional wood furniture.   #11 was our particular favorite.

POUSADA DE SAO TEOTONIO
4930 Valenca do Minho, Portugal
tel: 21-22252 telex: 32837
12 rooms - Moderate
Credit cards: all major
Restaurant, Excellent views
U.S. Rep: Marketing Ahead
Rep. tel: (212) 686-9213
Nearest airport: Porto (110 km)
Nearest train station: Valenca do Minho

This stylish turn-of-the-century inn crowns and shares a wooded hill with the striking, contemporary pilgrimage church of the same name.   They both also share a spectacular view of the small port town of Viana hugging the banks of the Lima River.   The large, pale-stone hotel has recently reopened after extensive renovation which transformed it from well-worn comfort to streamlined elegance.   The decor retains the best of the original old-world flavor, but interior designers have added unique spice.   You'll discover grand-scale public rooms with handsome, pastel-upholstered furniture, and broad hallways with high, French ceilings and natural parquet floors which provide a delightful framework for sleek Scandinavian-style tables accented with fanciful art-deco lamps and mirrors.   The theme is continued in the spacious bedrooms, which have natural-wood beds with leather-strip headboards, pale brown carpet, soft brown chairs and glass tables.   Be sure to request one of the many rooms that overlook the church and river.   A wide verandah and the dining room also enjoy the extensive panorama.   An oval swimming pool is encircled by trees.   Although not called a pousada, the hotel is run by that government chain.

HOTEL DE SANTA LUZIA
Monte de Santa Luzia
4900 Viana do Castelo, Portugal
tel: 58-22192 telex: 32420
47 rooms - Moderate
Credit cards: all major
Restaurant, Pool
U.S. Rep: Marketing Ahead
Rep. tel: (212) 686-9213
Nearest airport: Porto (70 km)
Nearest train station: Viana do Castelo (5 km)

Tucked atop a hill overlooking the deep blue waters of the Canicada dam is a turn-of-the-century mountain lodge.   Once a private home, the ivy-covered, blue-shuttered stone building is now an attractive pousada situated within the Peneda-Geres National Park, one of Europe's most impressive nature reserves. Only the lounge and restaurant are to be found on the main floor, to either side of an open stone fireplace which reaches up to a wood-beamed cathedral ceiling. The cozy lounge and tiny bar are furnished in wood and pale leather.   The Swiss-style restaurant has fresh flowers on every table and floor-to-ceiling windows that overlook the lake surrounded by rich green, terraced hillsides.   An open stairway leads upstairs to the small, spotless bedrooms, with wood floors and four-poster single beds with leather headboards and brightly colored spreads.   A few of the rooms also have handsome, varnished wood-plank ceilings.   Most of the bedrooms overlook the courtyard and the tennis court, above which is a terrace with a large swimming pool and shaded tables.   But we suggest you request one of the premium bedrooms that have small wood balconies and lovely views over the water.

POUSADA DE SAO BENTO
4850 Vieira do Minho, Portugal
tel: 23-57190, telex: 32339
18 rooms - Moderate
Credit cards: all major
Restaurant, Pool, Good views
U.S. Rep: Marketing Ahead
Rep. tel: (212) 686-9213
Nearest airport: Porto (84 km)
Nearest train station: Braga (34 km)

This pousada, named after the 14th-century king who fortified the town against possible Spanish aggression, offers among the most unique accommodations in Portugal.   It is not well-marked, so watch carefully for it across from the big church on the main town square.   With the exception of the reception, housed in an old mansion, the inn is entirely installed within the ancient ramparts.   In fact, the pousada's public rooms and guestrooms are incorporated into the original dwellings that, until 1975, were inhabited by townsfolk.   Once you've settled in, don't fail to visit the tiny, 18th-century chapel with its ornate, painted ceiling and wood-slat floors.   Just behind an old pillory is a white-plaster and stone-framed manor home containing the hotel bar, lounge and sitting rooms, with wood floors and cozy leather furniture.   The spacious, attractive bedrooms are located in several separate buildings - remodelled village houses - and feature pale-wood, carved beds with woven wheat-colored spreads, soft brown carpet and brocade chairs.   Another building houses the breakfast room - on a lower level encircled by exposed fortifications - and the dining room, on the upper level with tall windows overlooking the Minho River.

POUSADA DE DOM DINIZ
Praca da Liberdade
4920 Vila Nova da Cerveira, Portugal
tel: 51-95601 telex: 32821
29 rooms - Expensive
Credit cards: all major
Restaurant, Medieval fortified town
U.S. Rep: Marketing Ahead
Rep. tel: (212) 686-9213
Nearest airport: Porto (107 km)
Nearest train station: Vila Nova da Cerveira

In the mid-17th century King Joao IV, formerly the Duke of Braganca, built a tiny stone castle in the remote fishing village of Vila Nova de Milfontes, overlooking the placid Mira River. For centuries it entertained royalty and nobility from throughout Portugal and Europe, but the post-revolutionary economy has motivated numerous families to open their homes to tourists, this one among them. You'll find the unmarked, ivy-covered castle, complete with dry moat and drawbridge, by driving through town to the water's edge (or by asking). As long as you've made reservations (a must), don't be put off by the "Private Property" sign on the iron gates. Just ring the bell on the massive wood door and be prepared to be admitted to spectacular and totally unique accommodations. Tall stone pillars support the ceiling in the foyer, which leads to the living room, small bar and dining room, exquisitely decorated with family heirlooms. All three meals come with the your lodging, are served at one heavy, dark-wood table, and are reputed to be marvellous. Narrow stone steps lead up to stone hallways, off which are smallish bedrooms, handsomely appointed with antiques. There is a beautiful, arcaded and ivy-draped terrace in back overlooking the water. The guestbook is replete with laudatory descriptions of others' visits here, and yours is guaranteed to be just as unforgettable.

CASTELO DE MILFONTES
Vila Nova de Milfontes, Portugal
tel: 83-96108
7 rooms - Moderate
Credit cards: none
Rate includes meals, 17th-century castle
Nearest airport: Lisbon (193 km)
Nearest train station: Santiago do Cacem (38 km)

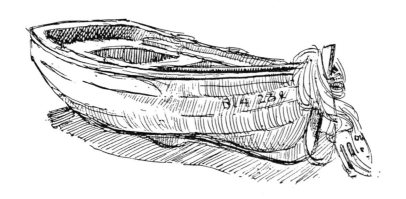

196

Accommodation in Private Homes

Relative to the rest of Europe, tourism is a new industry in Portugal. Scarcely a dozen years have passed since the 25th of April Revolution, and barely a decade since the installation of a moderate government which was externally perceived as stable. To make up for the shortfall of accommodation created by a renewed interest in travel in Portugal, the national tourist industry has begun to subsidize private-sector investment in the provision of travel lodging.

Due to these specific, basically political, circumstances, there exists in Portugal a unique sort of accommodation available to visitors. Unfortunately, because the concept is young and still under development, information regarding it is not readily available to tourists - in fact, to our knowledge, no comprehensive listing of such lodging exists outside of Portuguese literature save our own. Curiously enough, the National Tourist Office and Turismo de Habitacao (which translates roughly as "tourism in private houses"), the organizations behind the development of this singular industry, have no particular name for it. The closest we can come to a generic description is guest house, accomodation not unlike "bed and breakfast" lodging in Britain. We arrived at this nomenclature because the 129, so-far-established "guest houses" have two things in common: they are privately owned and occupied, and they offer rooms to tourists. The quarters accessible under this national program vary widely - from "casas rusticas" (rural homes), to "casas antigas" (historic homes), to solares (estates) - in ascending order of cost, generally.

As you might expect, the majority of such accommodation are situated in traditionally less-frequented areas, namely northern Portugal (the Costa Verde, in particular) and the mountainous regions, although some stellar examples are to be found in the Costa de Lisboa, the Costa de Prata and the Algarve.

However, be advised that a frame of mind and sense of adventure above and beyond the ordinary is required if you want to experience staying in a private home, not only because necessary information is scarce, and the proprietors may or may not speak English, but because a certain behavior is expected of you as a guest, precisely because you are staying in a private home. Meals (aside from breakfast, which is always included), if served, are often taken at a common table at a set hour and courtesy requires that you inform your host if you don't plan to partake. The same courtesy applies if you plan to arrive at or return to the guest house at an irregular hour. Reservations MUST be made a minimum of three days in advance, and they are most easily obtained through one of two national offices whose address is on page 204. These Tourismo de Habitacao offices will also provide invaluable directions to the guest houses (their off-the-beaten-track locations sometimes make them difficult to find).

As long as you bear these distinctions in mind, a stay in one or several of these private homes is guaranteed to furnish you with a memorable holiday because you will have the opportunity to experience Portuguese life as it is lived. Such accommodation simply cannot be compared to those offered by commercial hotels - nor do they endeavor to compete in many regards - but if you seek the reward of the out of the ordinary, this could be your cup of tea.

Accommodation in Private Homes

The list is organized in the following form: HOUSE NAME,   Mailing Address, (Area Code) Phone Number.   Often the town in the mailing address is not near the guesthouse.   In this case we have included the name of the town that the guest house is in, or nearest to, in brackets after the phone number.   Where no town name appears, the house is in or near the town in the mailing address.   The guest houses marked with an asterisk are those we have seen, and are described in the hotel section.   The list is divided into regions.   The Tourismo de Habitacao offices through which to obtain reservations are on page 204.

COSTA VERDE (area north of Porto):

CASA DE MIRAMAR, 4900 Afife, (58)91329
CASA AVELAR, 4970 Arcos de Valdevez, (58)65228, [Cabreiro]
PACO DA GLORIA,* 4970 Arcos de Valdevez, (58)941477, [Jolda]
CASA DO REQUEIJO, 4970 Arcos de Valdevez, (58)65272
QUINTA DE VALVERDE, 4970 Arcos de Valdevez, (58)66154
CASA DOS ASSENTOS, 4750 Barcelos, (1)218-4773, [Quintiaes]
CASA DO MONTE, 4750 Barcelos, (53)82519, [Abade de Neiva]
QUINTA DA BELA VISTA, 4700 Braga, (53)24563, [Bom Jesus]
CASA DA GRANJA, 4860 Cabeceiras de Basto, (2)485320, [Vila Nune]
CASA DO BARAO DE FERMIL, 4890 Celorico do Basto, (2)680778, [Fermil/Veade]
CASA DA ANTA, 4910 Caminha, (58)921434, [Lanhelas]
CASA DE ESTEIRO, 4910 Caminha, (58)921356
CASINHA DA FRAGA, 4910 Caminha, (1)662471
CASA DO RIBEIRO, 4800 Guimaraes, (53)410881, [S. Cristovao de Selho]
PACO DE S. CIPRIANO, 4800 Guimaraes, (53)481337, [Tabuadelo]
CASA DAS MARINHAS, 4740 Marinhas, (2)488841
CASA DO PADEIRO, 4950 Moncao, (2)683223
CASA DE RODAS, 4950 Moncao, (51)52105
CASA DE CEPEDA, 4580 Paredes, (55)26315
CASA DO REQUEIXO, 4830 Povoa de Lanhoso, (53)93112, [Frades]

CASA DE ABADES, 4990 Ponte de Lima, (58)941627, [S. Martinho de Gandara]
QUINTA DA ALDEIA, 4990 Ponte de Lima, (58)941132, [Crasto/Ribeiro]
CASA DE ANTEPACO, 4990 Ponte de Lima, (58)941702
CASA DE ARRABALDE, 4990 Ponte de Lima, (58)941106
CASA DE ARRIFANA, 4990 Ponte de Lima, (58)941131, [Moreira de Lima]
QUINTA DA BAIA, 4990 Ponte de Lima, (58)22699, [Gaifar]
CASA DO BARREIRO, 4990 Ponte de Lima, (58)941937, [Gemieira]
CASA DE BRUFE, 4990 Ponte de Lima, (58)942335, [Vitorino das Donas]
PACO DE CALHEIROS,* 4990 Ponte de Lima, (58)941364, [Calheiros]
CASTELO DE CORUTELO, 4990 Ponte de Lima, (58)961133, [S.Juliao de Freixo]
CASA DE COVAS, 4990 Ponte de Lima, (58)32109, [Moreira de Lima]
MOINHO DE ESTORAOS, 4990 Ponte de Lima, (58)942372, [Estoraos]
CASA DE SAO GONZALO, 4990 Ponte de Lima, (58)942365
CASA DE NAVAIA, 4990 Ponte de Lima, (58)941480, [S. Martinho de Gandara]
CASA DO OUTEIRO, 4990 Ponte de Lima, (58)941206, [Arcozelo]
CASA DAS PEREIRAS, 4990 Ponte de Lima, (58)941223
QUINTA DE SABADAO, 4990 Ponte de Lima, (58)941963
CASA DO SALGUEIRINHO, 4990 Ponte de Lima, (58)941206
CASA DO TAMANQUEIRO, 4990 Ponte de Lima, (58)942372, [Estoraos]
CASA DE CRASTO,* 4990 Ponte de Lima, (58)941156
CASA DAS TORRES, 4990 Ponte de Lima, (58)941369, [Facha]
CASA DE SILVADE, 4780 Santo Tirso, (52)53533, [Areias]
CASA DO AMEAL, 4900 Viana do Castelo, (58)22402, [Meadela]
PACO DE ANHA, 4900 Viana do Castelo, (58)28458, [Anha]
SOLAR DE CORTEGACA, 4900 Viana do Castelo, (58)971639, [Subportela]
CASA GRANDE DA BANDEIRA, 4900 Viana do Castelo, (58)23169
CASA DO OUTEIRO DE MORES, 4850 Vieira do Minho, (53)24986, [Outeiro de Mores]
CASA DA CRUZ REAL, 4850 Vieira do Minho, (53)57452, [Canicada]
QUINTA DO MAR, 4400 Vila Nova de Gaia, (2)302713, [Praia de Salgueiros]
QUINTA DAS TONGAS, 4730 Vila Verde, (53)32143

Accommodation in Private Homes

MONTANHAS (area between Coimbra and Porto and Spain):

CASA ZE DA CALCADA, 4600 Amarante, (55)422023, [Cepelos]
QUINTA DA PONTE, 6360 Celorico da Beira, (1)685597, [Faia]
QUINTA DA BOAVISTA, 5180 Freixo de Espada a Cinta, (2)682528
CASA DO BALCAO, 6230 Fundao, (75)57363, [Castelo Novo]
CASA DO BARREIRO, 6230 Fundao, (75)57120, [Alpedrinha]
CASA DE CIMA, 6230 Fundao, (75)57309, [Castelo Novo]
CASA DO OITAO, 6290 Gouveia, (38)42688, [Pacos da Serra]
CASA RAINHA, 6290 Gouveia, (38)42132, [Toural]
QUINTA DE SAO JOSE, 6000 Guarda, (71)96210, [Aldeia Vicosa]
SOLAR DAS ARCAS, 5340 Macedo de Cavaleiros, No Phone, [Arcas]
CASA DE GRIJO, 5340 Macedo de Cavaleiros, (71)42575
CASA DE SAO ROQUE, 6260 Manteigas, (75)47125
CASA DA CORREDOURA, 3520 Nelas, (1)683289, [Vilar Seco]
QUINTA DO VALE DO CHAO, 3520 Nelas, (32)94319, [Santar]
CASA MAGALHAES COUTINHO, 3550 Penalva do Castelo, (32)64219
CASA DE VARAIS, 5050 Peso da Regua, (54)23251, [Cambres]
QUINTA DA FOZ, 5085 Pinhao, (54)72353
CASA DO CASAL, 4660 Resende, (1)540832, [Rendufe]
CASA DE SEBORDINHOS, 4870 Ribeira de Pena, (59)47218, [Serva]
CASA ARABE, 6320 Sabugal, (71)68129, [Sortelha]
CASA DO PALHEIRO, 6320 Sabugal, (71)68182, [Sortelha]
CASA DO VENTO QUE SOA, 6320 Sabugal, (71)68182, [Sortelha]
CASAS DO CRUZEIRO, 6270 Seia, (38)22825, [Sabugueiro]
CASA DA PONTE, 6270 Seia, (38)93253, [Alvoco da Serra]
CASA DE REBORDINHO, 3500 Viseu, (32)21258, [Rebordinho]

COSTA DE PRATA (area between Obidos and Aveiro):

CASA DA PADEIRA, 2460 Alcobaca, (62)48272, [Aljubarrota]
SOLAR DA VACARICA, 3050 Mealhada, (31)93458, [Vacarica]
CASAL DA CANASTRA, 2510 Obidos, No Phone.
CASA DAS MARES, 2520 Peniche, (62)75199, [Praia do Baleal]
QUINTA DO RIO ALCAIDE, 2480 Porto de Mos, (44)42124
QUINTA DO HESPANHOL, 2575 Runa, (61)73209, [Carreiras]
CASA DO CARVALHAL, 2560 Torres Vedras, (61)95466, [Carvalhal]
CASAL DO GIL, 2560 Torres Vedras, (61)91184, [Ermigeira]
QUINTA DE SAO JOSE, 2590 Sobral de Monte Agraco, (61)94133

COSTA DE LISBOA (area from Setubal to Sintra):

QUINTA DA PRAIA, 2890 Alcochete, (1)661648
QUINTA DA FONTE NOVA, 2735 Cacem, (1)926-0021, [Rio de Mouro]
CASA DA PERGOLA, 2750 Cascais, (1)284-0040
CASA DA ROCHEIRA, 2765 Estoril, (1)268-1094
CASA DA LAPA, 1200 Lisboa, (1)602727
CASA DA ARQUITECTA, 2970 Sesimbra, (1)548265
CASA DA NOSSA SENHORA, 2970 Sesimbra, (1)771984
QUINTA DA CAPELA, 2710 Sintra, (1)923-0210
QUINTA DE SAO TIAGO,* 2710 Sintra, (1)923-2923
QUINTA DE SANTO ANDRE, 2600 Vila Franca de Xira, (63)22776

Accommodation in Private Homes

PLANICIES (between the Algarve and Lisbon and Spain):

QUINTA DOS VALES, 2200 Abrantes, (41)97363, [Tramagal]
CASA DOS CEDROS, 2025 Alcanede, (1)800986
HERDADE DE ALMARGEM, 7400 Arraiolos, (66)42443
PALACIO DE CONSTANCIA, 2250 Constancia, (49)93371
CASA DE SANTA BARBARA, 2250 Constancia, (1)872080
CASA DO CONDE DA SERRA, 7000 Evora, (66)31257
CONVENTO DE SAO PAULO, 7170 Redondo, (66)99415, [Serra de Ossa]
CASA DO CASTELO, 7200 Reguengos de Monsaraz, (66)55136
CASA DA CUMEADA, 7200 Reguengos de Monasaraz, (66)56109, [Cumeada]
CASA DOM NUNO, 7200 Reguengos de Monsaraz, (66)55146
CASA DA PALMEIRA, 7200 Reguengos de Monsaraz, (66)52362
CASAL DA TORRE, 2000 Santarem, (43)76227
HORTA DO AVO, 2350 Torres Novas, (49)91116, [Soudos]
MOINHO DO LOURAL, 2560 Torres Vedras, (1)993-5505
MOINHO DA ASNEIRA, 7555 Cercal do Alentejo, (83)96267, [Vila Nova de Milfontes]
QUINTA DO MOINHO DO VENTO, 7555 Cercal do Alentejo, (83)96383,
    [Vila Nova de Milfontes]
CASA DOS ARCOS, 7160 Vila Vicosa, (68)42518

ALGARVE (extreme south):

CASA DO MATO, 8200 Albufeira, (1)247-3614
CASA DA BELA MOURA, 8400 Lagoa, (82)33422, [Porches]
CASA DA ALFARROBEIRA, 8600 Lagos, No Phone, [Odiaxere]
CASA DO PINHAO, 8600 Lagos, (82)62371
CASA DA PAZ, 8550 Monchique, (82)92576
QUINTA DA SOBREIRA, 2035 Pernes, (43)42444
CASA DAS TRES PALMEIRAS, 8500 Portimao, (82)22275, [Praia do Vau]
QUINTA DO CARACOL, 8800 Tavira, (81)22475

TOURISMO DE HABITACAO OFFICES

Reservation office for guest houses in the Costa Verde area:

Delegacao de Turismo de Ponte de Lima
4990 Ponte de Lima, Portugal
Tel: (58)942335, Telex: 32618

Reservation office for guest houses in ALL BUT the Costa Verde area:

Direccao-Geral de Turismo
Turismo de Habitacao
Rua Alexandre Herculano, 51-3.o dt.o
1200 Lisboa, Portugal
Tel: (1)681713

Accommodation in Private Homes

HOTEL NAME & ADDRESS - clearly printed or typed

Exmos. senhores:

Escrevemos para fazer uma reserva para _____ noite(s)
We are writing to make a reservation for (number of) night(s)

desde o dia _____ de _____ ate o dia _____ de _____
from   (date) of (month)   to   (date) of   (month).
(months are JANEIRO, FEVEREIRO, MARCO, ABRIL, MAIO, JUNHO,
JULHO, AGOSTO, SETEMBRO, OUTUBRO, NOVEMBRO, DEZEMBRO)

_____quarto(s) individual(ais)   com cama extra - with an extra bed
     single room(s)   com vista do mar - with a sea view
                                   com terraco - with a terrace
_____quarto(s) duplo(s)   com banho - with bath
     double room(s)   num andar alto - on an upper floor
                                   num andar baixo - on a lower floor
_____suite(s)   a frente - in the front
     suite(s)   atras - in the back

Somos _____ pessoas.
We have (number of) persons in our party.

Tenha a bondade de avisar sobre se e disponivel o quarto, o preco dele, e se e
preciso uma garantia. Esperando a sua resposta, subscrevemo-nos
atenciosamente,

Please advise availability, the rate and the deposit necessary. Awaiting your
reply, we remain, sincerely,

YOUR NAME & ADDRESS - clearly printed or typed

Index - Alphabetically by Hotel

HOTEL	TOWN	PAGE #
PALACE HOTEL DO BUCACO	Bucaco	103, 149
PALACIO DE SETEAIS, Hotel	Sintra	187
PALOMA BLANCA, Hotel	Aveiro	110, 145
PARQUE, Hotel	Sao Martinho do Porto	100, 184
PRINCIPE REAL, Hotel	Lisbon	163
QUINTA DE SAO THIAGO	Sintra	188
QUINTA DAS TORRES	Azeitao	52, 146
RAINHA SANTA ISABEL, Pda.	Estremoz	94, 155
RAINHA SANTA ISABEL, Alb.	Obidos	174
DA RIA, Pda.	Murtosa	170
DE SANTA LUZIA, Pda.	Elvas	77, 154
SANTA LUZIA, Hotel	Viana do Castelo	140, 192
DE SANTA MARIA, Pda.	Marvao	92, 166
SANTA MARINHA DA COSTA, Pda.	Guimaraes	124, 160
DE SAO BENTO, Pda.	Vieira do Minho	126, 193
DE SAO BRAS, Pda.	Sao Bras de Alportel	183
DE SAO FILIPE, Pda.	Setubal	186
DE SAO LORENCO, Pda.	Manteigas	108, 165
DE SAO PEDRO, Pda.	Tomar-Castelo de Bode	91, 189
DE SAO TEOTONIO, Pda.	Valenca do Minho	138, 191
DE SAO TIAGO, Pda.	Santiago do Cacem	56, 182
DA SENHORA DA GUIA, Est.	Cascais	153
URGEIRICA, Hotel	Urgeirica	190
VILA JOYA	Guia	158
VILA LIDO, Alb.	Portimao	177
YORK HOUSE	Lisbon	164

Index - Alphabetically by Town

TOWN	HOTEL	PAGE#
MURTOSA	Pda. da Ria	170
OBIDOS	Pda. do Castelo	171
OBIDOS	Est. do Convento	83, 172
OBIDOS	Mansao da Torre	173
OBIDOS	Albergaria Rainha Sta. Isabe	174
PALMELA	Pda. do Castelo de Palmela	70, 175
PONTE DE LIMA	Casa de Crasto	176
PORTIMAO	Albergaria Vila Lido	177
PORTO	Hotel Infante de Sagres	113, 178
SAGRES	Fortaleza do Beliche	179
SAGRES	Pda. do Infante	58, 180
SANTA BARBARA DE NEXE	Hotel La Reserve	64, 181
SANTIAGO DO CACEM	Pda. de Sao Tiago	56, 182
SAO BRAS DE ALPORTEL	Pda. de Sao Bras	183
SAO MARTINHO DO PORTO	Hotel Parque	100, 184
SERRA	Est. da Ilha do Lombo	185
SETUBAL	Pda. de Sao Filipe	186
SINTRA	Hotel Palacio de Seteais	187
SINTRA	Quinta de Sao Thiago	188
TOMAR-CASTELO DE BODE	Pda. de Sao Pedro	91, 189
URGEIRICA	Hotel Urgeirica	190
VALENCA DO MINHO	Pda. de Sao Teotonio	138, 191
VIANA DO CASTELO	Hotel Santa Luzia	140, 192
VIEIRA DO MINHO	Pda. de Sao Bento	126, 193
VILA NOVA DA CERVEIRA	Pda. de Dom Diniz	194
VILA NOVA DE MILFONTES	Castelo de Milfontes	195

Inn Discoveries From Our Readers

Future editions of KAREN BROWN'S COUNTRY INN GUIDES TO EUROPE are going to include a new feature - a list of hotels recommended by our readers. We have received many letters describing wonderful inns you have discovered; however, we have never included them until we had the opportunity to make a personal inspection. This seemed a waste of some marvelous "tips". Therefore, in order to feature them we have decided to add a new section called "Inn Discoveries from Our Readers".

If you have a favorite discovery you would be willing to share with other travelers who love to travel the "inn way", please let us hear from you and include the following information:

1. Your name, address and telephone number.

2. Name, address and telephone of "Your Inn".

3. Brochure or picture of inn (we cannot return photographs).

4. Written permission to use an edited version of your description.

5. Would you want your name, city and state included in the book?

In addition to our current guide books, we are also researching future books in Europe and updating those previously published. We would appreciate comments on any of your favorites. The type of inn we would love to hear about are those with special "Olde Worlde" ambiance, charm and atmosphere. We need a brochure or picture so that we can select those which most closely follow the mood of our guides. We look forward to hearing from you. Thank you very much!

TRAVEL PRESS – KAREN BROWN'S
Country Inn Guides To Europe

The most reliable & informative series on European Country Inns

Detailed itineraries guide you through the countryside and suggest a cozy inn for
each night's stay. In the hotel section every listing has been inspected and
chosen for its special ambiance. Charming accommodations reflect every price range
from budget hideaways to deluxe palaces.

ORDER FORM

If you would like to receive an additional copy or purchase other books in Karen Brown's series on European country inns, the following books can be purchased in bookstores or ordered directly from the publisher. The individual country guides are all similar in style and format. They include detailed countryside itineraries with maps and a section describing captivating hotels. These guides enhance any travel library and make wonderful gifts.

....

KAREN BROWN'S COUNTRY INN GUIDES TO EUROPE

AUSTRIAN COUNTRY INNS & CASTLES $10.95
EUROPEAN COUNTRY CUISINE, ROMANTIC INNS & RECIPES $10.95
ENGLISH, WELSH & SCOTTISH COUNTRY INNS $10.95
FRENCH COUNTRY INNS & CHATEAUX $10.95
GERMAN COUNTRY INNS & CASTLES $10.95
ITALIAN COUNTRY INNS & VILLAS $10.95
PORTUGESE COUNTRY INNS & POUSADAS $10.95
SCANDINAVIAN COUNTRY INNS & MANORS $10.95
SPANISH COUNTRY INNS & PARADORS $10.95
SWISS COUNTRY INNS & CHALETS $9.95

Add $1.50 per copy for postage & handling. California residents add sales tax.

Indicate the number of copies of each title. Send in form with your check to:

TRAVEL PRESS
P.O. BOX 70
SAN MATEO, CA 94401
(415) 342-9117

NAME _____STREET _____

CITY _____ STATE _____ ZIP _____

KAREN BROWN traveled to France when she was nineteen and wrote "French Country Inns and Chateau Hotels" - the first book of what has grown to be an extremely successful series on European country inns. With nine books now on the market, Karen's staff has expanded, but she is still involved in the planning, research, formatting and editing each of the guides in her Country Inn series. Karen, her husband, Rick, and their daughter live in the San Francisco Bay area. When not writing, her hobbies include collecting antiques, skiing, cooking, entertaining and, of course, playing with her baby daughter, Alexandra.

CYNTHIA and RALPH KITE admit to a long-term love affair with Europe where they have lived and traveled extensively over the last 14 years. Both are intimately acquainted with the culture and customs of the Iberian Peninsula. Ralph is a Professor of Hispanic Literature at a major American university and has authored several texts on the culture and language of the Spanish-speaking world. Cynthia has always had an interest in language and travel and has studied in Mexico, Spain and France. She holds a degree in Spanish and French, and is currently pursuing a successful publishing career as Production Director for a national magazine. Together, Cynthia and Ralph have visited almost every Latin country in the world and have traveled throughout Europe - west and east - as well as South America.

BARBARA TAPP is the talented young artist responsible for the interior sketches and cover painting for "Portuguese Country Inns and Pousadas". Raised in Australia, Barbara studied in Sydney at The School of Interior Design. Before coming to the United States, Barbara worked as an exhibition designer for the Sydney Taronga Zoo. Although Barbara continues with freelance projects, she devotes most of her time to illustrating Karen's European Country Inn guides. Like Karen, Barbara shares a fondness for travel and has lived in Europe. Her knowledge and love of the countryside add greatly to the charm of her delightful sketches. Barbara now lives in the San Francisco Bay area with her husband, Richard, and their young sons, Jonathon and Alexander.

This guide is especially written for individual travelers who want to plan their own vacations. However, should you prefer to join a group and have all of the details of your holiday preplanned, Town and Country Travel Service can recommend tours using country inns with romantic ambiance for many of the nights' accommodations. Or, should you want to organize your own group (art class, gourmet society, bridge club, etc.) and travel with friends, Town and Country Travel Service will customize a tour for you using small hotels with special charm and appeal.

For further information please call:

TOWN & COUNTRY TRAVEL SERVICE
16 East Third Avenue
San Mateo, CA 94401

Within California 800-227-6734
Outside California 800-227-6733